TH]

THE OLD RELIGION

An Examination into the Facts
of the English Reformation

by

J. L. C. DART

WIPF & STOCK · Eugene, Oregon

Wipf and Stock Publishers
199 W 8th Ave, Suite 3
Eugene, OR 97401

The Old Religion
An Examination into the Facts of the English Reformation
By Dart, J. L. C.
Copyright©1956 SPCK
ISBN 13: 978-1-4982-9499-7
Publication date 5/14/2016
Previously published by SPCK, 1956

TO
GWENDOLINE
MY VERY DEAR
WIFE

CONTENTS

FOREWORD

I AM partially responsible for the appearance of this book. One day, some years ago, I remarked to Canon Dart that it was high time that the people of this country recognized that the Church of England is the true Catholic Church of this land, and that a book should be written to emphasize this point; the book has now been written. It is my hope that it will have a wide circulation.

Constant travel among the men of the three Armed Services during the past six and a half years, has convinced me that there is widespread ignorance of the Faith. Men do not know the facts. They fail to recognize that Roman Catholics have no right to usurp the word "Catholic". When a Roman Catholic calls himself a Catholic he implies that non-Romans are not Catholic. He endeavours to place Anglicans under the one title "Protestant" together with members of other denominations. This is unfair to the Anglican Church, as Canon Dart convincingly points out. Since the Reformation we have never ceased to be Catholics. Indeed, since we believe that Catholic Dogma rests upon the Bible and that certain recent Dogmas promulgated by Papal authority are unbiblical, we believe that we have adhered more closely to the true Catholic faith than have those who accept Papal Infallibility.

Controversy is distasteful, but the presentation of Truth is salutary. Canon Dart has presented his case with clarity and fair-mindedness.

I hope that this book will remove erroneous beliefs about the Church of England and challenge her members to a more militant faith.

†CUTHBERT COVENTRY

PREFACE

THIS BOOK is not anti-anybody or anything. It is not written to attack the faith, or the customs, of men who are not members of the Church of England. It is pro-Church of England. It is my most sincere belief that the Church of England is the Catholic Church in my country. Although I detest the chaos which exists within it at the present moment, I still believe that it holds the secret which must inspire the Catholic Church of the future. The problem which faces us is how to combine authority and order with liberty. It is a shockingly difficult thing to do. Much of the Catholic Church has given up the task as impossible. Rome certainly has, and what a wonderful unity she has achieved. But at what a cost! Not only has freedom of expression been destroyed, but freedom of thought also. Whenever the Sovereign Pontiff issues an important decree it is not lawful to oppose it "even secretly" in the heart. The democratic method of persuasion through argument—which after all was the method pursued by the Universal Church in the days of the Great Councils—can never hope to achieve the "tidiness" of an autocracy. But it is the true method for men who are free and not slaves. St Paul exhorts us to "stand fast in the liberty wherewith Christ hath made us free" and although he is thinking about freedom from the bondage of the Jewish law, yet, so it seems to me, his words have a wider application.

The Reformation swept over West Europe like a great storm, and religion has never been the same since. That is true even in Roman Catholic countries. In some places Catholic organization and traditions were completely destroyed. In England much that was rotten with age was swept away and so also were many things that were profitable and lovely. But the ancient Church in our country was left standing on the old apostolic foundations. It was neither blown into the Protestant fold nor, as is so often stated, was it left balancing on a fence. It was left recognizably the Church which St Augustine and St Columba had founded, the continuing

xi

Church of England. The Book of Common Prayer contains the proof of this conviction and suggests how it is possible to combine authority with liberty, how to be Catholic without submission to autocracy.

My most grateful thanks are offered to the Bishop of Coventry for his Foreword and for much encouragement. Also to Father Bernard Wigan for his sympathy and for much helpful criticism. Once again I find it impossible to say how much I owe to Miss Dora Garside, for her willingness to wrestle with my abominable writing, to point out mistakes, to control a chaotic use of capital letters, to type and to re-type.

I should also like to make grateful acknowledgement to Mr. H. Bettenson and the Oxford University Press for permission to quote from his translations in *Documents of the Christian Church.*

J. L. C. DART

Dormans,
1956

CHAPTER 1

THE PURPOSE OF THIS BOOK

IN THE Middle Ages, it is universally agreed, the Church of England—that title is no Reformation invention; Magna Charta for example, speaks of the *Ecclesia Anglicana*—was an integral part of the Catholic Church. It comprised two provinces of the Western Church. It had some peculiarities of its own, but in all essentials it conformed to the general pattern of Christianity in the West, both in doctrine and practice. What happened at the Reformation? Like men always and everywhere, our reformers were dissimilar in holiness and in grasp of the meaning and purpose of the faith, and it is quite possible by careful selection from their writings to present a fairly convincing case for, or against, the orthodoxy of nearly all of them.

But that particular effort is futile. It does not in the very least matter what Henry VIII and Elizabeth, Gardiner and Cranmer, Cardinal Pole and Latimer, Campion and Parker believed. It does not matter what the reformers as individuals taught, or even what they tried to do. It is completely immaterial, for example, whether, as Dom Gregory Dix seemed to think, Cranmer in 1552 attempted to produce a Liturgy which expressed a Zwinglian view of the Eucharist or whether, as Humphrey Whitby used to maintain, his aim was the same as that of the Roman Liturgical Movement. The opinions of the reformers were their own and they have long ago gone to their rewards. What does matter is what they actually accomplished.

That is good law. Parliament hammers out an Act. The members of the government, which passes it, may not regard it with identical pleasure, but when once it is passed it is "law" and it comes to the Courts for enforcement. The lawyers never argue, for example, "This act was proposed by Mr Red and won the support of all the left-wing members. Therefore it must have an almost communistic meaning." That kind of argument is never heard in a court of law. What the lawyers ask is "what does this form of words actually say? What does it actually mean?" The supposed opinions of the legislators are not taken into account at all.

In the same way we are not concerned with the opinions of men in that revolutionary period of the Church's life called the Reformation. What does matter is—what did they do?

They left a Book of Common Prayer and an Ordinal as the only completely authoritative documents of the Church of England. It is to them that we must turn if we wish to know what actually happened at the Reformation. They come to us with the authority of both Convocation and Parliament. Every minister of the Church is commissioned with the forms of the Ordinal. Every priest swears to use the Prayer Book in all his public ministrations. It is by these two documents that the Church of England must be judged—by the actual words, and not by any theories about the opinions of their compilers. Is the Ordinal valid? Does the Prayer Book continue the system of the Catholic Church? If those two documents are in actual fact Catholic, and the breach with the Papacy was not vital, then the Church of England is the continuing Catholic Church of our country. Otherwise we belong to a Protestant sect which arose in the sixteenth century. This is the problem which we will consider in the following pages.

The method that will be pursued is this: First to state as clearly as possible the history and accepted Catholic teaching and practice about the custom or dogma under consideration. Then to examine the actual words of the Ordinal or Prayer Book, as the case may be, to see how far they agree, or disagree, with Catholic tradition on the subject. The Articles and opinions of accredited teachers will usually be considered only when they seem to contradict the Catholic interpretation of the letter of the law. The thesis which it is believed will be established is that the Church of England, far from being a new institution created at the Reformation, is the old historic Church of our country. It maintains the ancient Faith, continues the historic ministry, and administers the Catholic sacraments.

CHAPTER 2

THE HISTORICAL BACKGROUND

1. *The Schism*

WHEN did the Church of England begin? Did St Columba and St Augustine, or Henry VIII, start it on its way? Most certainly not Henry VIII. It may have become schismatic during his reign and it may have become heretical during the reign of his son, Edward VI. But Cranmer, consecrated archbishop in the reign of Henry VIII, received the pallium, which is the sign of papal recognition, from Pope Clement VII, and even in Roman eyes he remained the legitimate Archbishop of Canterbury until he was deposed from his Orders under Mary. Rome made no attempt to replace him until he had been killed. Under Mary it was not a new body, but the old *Ecclesia Anglicana*, which was reconciled to the Papacy. A Christian is a man who has been baptized. If he falls into sin he does not cease to be a Christian. If he repents he is not baptized again; he is absolved. Under Mary the Church of England was not, so to speak, re-baptized, or reconstituted a Church. The Pope sent to it a legate, Cardinal Pole, who solemnly absolved it and restored it to unity with the Papacy. It is only a Catholic who can be absolved. Pole absolved a continuing Catholic Church; a body which had continued part of the Church in spite of all the supposedly schismatic or heretical things that had been done under Henry VIII and Edward VI. In the eyes of Roman Catholics, when Mary came to the throne the Church was there, although it did not function properly until restored to union with the Papacy by Cardinal Pole. Then, after the death of Mary, Elizabeth became Queen. The Papacy tried hard to persuade her to return to the papal allegiance, going so far, as we shall see,[1] as to propose to authorize the Prayer Book, in return for the acceptance of the papal supremacy. When blandishments failed other

[1] Cf. p. 190.

3

methods were tried. The Queen was pronounced illegitimate and deposed and all her subjects were ordered to disobey her.[1] That was in 1570. The Bull was followed by plots against the Queen's life, Jesuit intrigues in England, rebellions in Ireland, and by the Spanish Armada in 1588. It was the publication of this Bull, excommunicating the Queen and all her subjects who remained faithful to her, which marked the beginning of a new order. Not until 1588 were there two separate, hostile, organizations in England, both claiming to be the Catholic Church, and the question arose for the first time—which is the Catholic Church in England?

2. The Preliminary Stages of the Reformation

Like all historical events, the final separation of Canterbury from Rome was the culmination of a long movement. There were three distinct stages: (1.) The political reformation marked by the first successful abolition of the papal supremacy by Henry VIII. (2.) The doctrinal reformation of the reign of Edward VI. (3.) The modification and consolidation of both in the settlement achieved under Elizabeth.

Henry VIII's repudiation of the papal jurisdiction in England was novel, only because it was successful. His action involved the prohibition of all appeals to the Pope and the rejection of all papal claims to universal jurisdiction and authority over the Church in England. These things were implicit in the acts of William I, when he refused the homage the Pope demanded, and decreed that no Pope should be recognized in any part of his dominions "except at his own order, and that no one should receive from him any communication whatsoever, unless it was first shown to himself", that no ecclesiastical order or prohibition should be promulgated apart from his command, and that no one should be tried in any ecclesiastical court, censured or excommunicated for any sin or crime, "except at his own bidding".[2] Henry II took up the

---

[1] Henry VIII had been excommunicated and his subjects forbidden to obey him. That was in 1535. But this Bull was never published and in consequence it could not have affected the Church and nation. For the words of the Bulls see Chap. 16.

[2] Eadmer, *History*, Vol. I, p. 6.

same attitude in the Constitutions of Clarendon, and he added rules of great importance, the chief of them being that no archbishop or bishop should leave the kingdom (to go to the Pope) without his permission; that appeals from ecclesiastical courts should be to the bishop, then to the archbishop, and "if the archbishop shall fail in administering justice" to the King, thus barring the appeal to the Pope. All bishoprics and abbacies and priories, being vacant, are to be in the King's "hand" and he shall receive all their revenues. Elections to fill the vacancies are to be held in the King's chapel, with his consent, and by persons he summons for that purpose. The King is to "recommend the best person" to be elected.

It is clear that all this legislation created exactly the same position as that which Henry VIII was to establish later, except for one thing. The Pope was left with a titular headship. But although Henry II left the Pope his titles, he claimed all his powers and, if he had had his way, the Church of England would have become as early as 1163 the autonomous national Church that the Reformation made it.[1]

That was the aim of Henry II, a Church and State equally subject to the Crown. He failed in his endeavour for three reasons. The spiritual prestige of the Papacy was very great. Pope Alexander III, with whom Henry II had to deal, was both a good and a great man. Secondly, the Church was regarded by the people of England as their main shield against irresponsible tyranny. It alone stood between the poor and the rapacity of the baronial class and the inhumanity of royal officials. Lastly, the English nation had not yet emerged. The King was a Frenchman and French was the language of the Court. The feudal system involved loyalty to a personal ruler, whatever his nationality, and the ideal of "my country" had not come into existence. When therefore Henry II made his great mistake and shocked the public conscience by his responsibility for the murder of Archbishop Becket, he made the defeat of his policy inevitable.

When Henry VIII embarked on the same policy he carried it through with scarcely any difficulty. As Sir Thomas More put it, all the bishops and leading clerical and lay persons of his kingdom

[1] The rights and wrongs of the royal supremacy are argued in Chap. 16.

2

signed "right merrily" the Act of Submission acknowledging the King as Supreme Head of the Church. There were a few who died rather than renounce the Pope, and there were some disturbances, such as the Pilgrimage of Grace. But the revolts were due in far greater measure to the economic difficulties, consequent upon the suppression of the monasteries, than to the anti-papal legislation. The change in public sentiment was due to the facts that by the time of Henry VIII a succession of worldly and vicious Popes had thrown away all spiritual prestige; the King, and not the Church, held the affection of the people; and England had emerged as a nation, intolerant of all foreign interference. The political Reformation which Henry VIII carried through in his lifetime succeeded because it was in accordance with the wishes and consciences of the great majority of Englishmen. In great measure the change in public opinion was due to a demoralized Papacy and an unworthy Church.

3. *The Government's Problem*

Soon after Elizabeth's succession to the throne the Duke of Norfolk reminded her, "Let your Highness assure yourself that England can bear no more changes in religion, it hath been bowed so oft that if it should be bent again it would break." The warning was unnecessary, for not Elizabeth nor her ministers nor her ecclesiastics had any desire for changes. Their main objective was not for any ideological conception of the Church, and its functions, but for freedom for it and the kingdom from all foreign control and entanglements. They wanted peace and order at home, and the stilling of religious controversy. This is stated very clearly in the Prefaces to the Book of Common Prayer.

Consider the position abroad. Spain was in the grasp of the Inquisition, the cruelty and ruthlessness of which shocked even the Papacy to protest. Germany was torn by religious dissensions and wars, which inflicted terrible suffering upon ordinary folk. In the Low Countries Alva was carrying on one of the most terrible reigns of terror ever known, and he bequeathed to his successors a bitter war of liberation, which was marked by the sacking of cities, murders, and torture, until it ended with the recognition of the independence of Holland. In France the attempt to settle the religious question by the Massacre of St Bartholomew in 1572 failed, and civil war between the Catholics and Huguenots became endemic. In all these disasters, political and economic questions played a part, but the standards under which men fought and murdered and plundered were religious. The assassins and the armies were organized as Catholics and Protestants. In Italy alone, although the troubles there were almost as widespread as elsewhere, dynastic and political issues were the main causes of contention. Is it possible to blame Elizabeth and her ministers for desiring to keep their country from being drawn into the orbit of these bloody disasters? There were two different sets of fanatics who would gladly have plunged England into the whirlpool. On the one side there was the papal party, eager for alliance with the Catholic powers, some of them prepared to assassinate the Queen, to foment rebellion in Ireland, and even to encourage a Spanish invasion. On the other side there were the extreme Protestants, led often by men who had learned their religion while exiles in Switzerland during the reign of Mary, who desired England to intervene actively on the side of Protestants everywhere. Each set of partisans was eager to purge England by "liquidating" the other.

In such circumstances what could the government do? To have espoused either side would have rent England with civil war and exhausted any strength that was left in foreign adventure. That way spelt national suicide. Instead Elizabeth tried to keep on as good terms as possible with the Catholic powers by dangling herself as a desirable bride for eligible Catholic princes, even for Philip of Spain, her deceased half-sister's husband. Of course England was the real bait which lured these royal suitors, but by flirting first with one and then another Elizabeth kept them from joining together to attack her country. So long as they were angling for the prize there could be nothing but jealousy between them. Also so long as there was any hope of a Catholic alliance, the papal party in England was comparatively content.

Comparatively—because some of them could not forget that Elizabeth was the issue of a marriage contracted, without dispensation, by Henry VIII, while his wife Catherine of Aragon was still alive. For anyone who valued the ancient disciplinary traditions, Anne Boleyn's marriage was invalid and Elizabeth was illegitimate. It was inevitable that strict Catholics should regard Mary, Queen of Scots as the legitimate Queen of England. That faith inspired the plots to assassinate Elizabeth, which were only brought to an end with the execution of her rival in 1587. But except for the small minority of firebrands, Elizabeth's policy of keeping the great Catholic powers divided by suggesting to them all in turn the possibility of a profitable alliance with England, served to satisfy the majority of the papal party in her kingdom until she had firmly established it in loyalty to herself. She played for time, and she won it.

The Pope struck in 1562 when he issued a brief forbidding Catholics to attend the services of the Church of England. In 1569 he published a Bull declaring Elizabeth a usurper of the English throne and absolving her subjects from their oaths of loyalty to her. In 1579 a papal force was landed in Ireland. In 1588 came the launching of the Spanish Armada. With its crushing defeat the danger from Rome and the Catholic powers passed away. France was in chaos. Spain's claws had been cut. The extremists in England had no focus for their agitation after the death of Mary Stuart, for no Englishman was prepared to exchange Elizabeth for Philip.

The danger that the government had now to face came from the extreme Protestants. From the beginning of Elizabeth's reign they had pressed for alliance with their co-religionists everywhere, and especially with William of Orange in the Low Countries and with the Huguenots in France. Even the Queen's ministers were mainly of the opinion that this was the wisest course. But Elizabeth would have none of it. She could not, however, afford to antagonize a party on whom she would be forced to rely if war should be declared by a Catholic power; therefore she played what was essentially the same game of "flirtation" with the insurgent Protestants of the Continent that she had played with the Catholic princes. She conciliated her own extreme Protestants by sending small sums of money to William of Orange and Condé to help them in their struggle and she sanctioned a few, very ineffective, landings by small expeditionary forces. She "looked the other way" when enthusiastic young Englishmen departed to serve in the Protestant armies, and she smiled graciously upon the privateers who preyed on the convoys carrying the sinews of war to the Spanish armies in the Low Countries. By honouring successful captains she pleased her Protestant subjects and built up the fleet and the enthusiasm, which was to destroy the Armada. But when that victory had been won the Protestant menace still remained.

4. *The Continuing Enemy*

When at last Spain had attempted invasion and failed, England had little more to fear from the Catholic powers. How to prevent the Protestant element in England from entangling the country in the cause of continental Protestantism then became the problem of foreign politics and, at home, the difficulty was how to restrain this element from antagonizing the great majority of the nation, who were conservative in all matters of religion. The greatness of this danger was apparent in wanton acts of destruction of what were called "superstitious objects" and in a bitter struggle to make Genevan standards of worship, and Calvinistic and Zwinglian articles of faith, the rule for the Church of England. The reality of this danger is proved by the fact that the bigoted Protestant minority of Elizabeth's reign grew into the Puritan party, which, two reigns later, fought a successful civil war, murdered a king and an archbishop, abolished episcopacy and the priesthood, and made the worship of the Church of England illegal. Roman controversialists often write as if the Church of England deliberately adopted Protestant standards. An attempt will be made to show, in detail, how false that is. The truth is that during all the revolution, which we call the Reformation, desperate attempts were made to break the continuity of the Church of England with its past and to replace the historic Church with a new body, formed on the pattern of Geneva and Zurich. The same attempt was made in Scotland and there, eventually, it succeeded.[1] Presbyterianism, or Congregationalism, which is a still further departure from the historic shape of the Church, were the systems which the extreme Protestants desired to impose on England. The

[1] Cf. Chap. 18.

thing was done in the great Swiss cantons, and in parts of France and Germany, in Holland and in Scotland. But the attempt failed in England. That failure is a fact.

The Church of England was not remade according to the Protestant pattern. But the issue was long in doubt. All through the latter part of Elizabeth's reign and through those of James I and Charles I the struggle went on. As this book progresses it will be seen how the battle was fought out in every department of the Church's life and practice. At this point it is necessary to emphasize no more than the fact that the Protestants were the real enemy. Rome was got rid of without much difficulty ; even the attempt to win back England to the papal obedience by enlisting the might of Spain proved a fiasco. But the struggle for the maintenance of Catholic order, for a sacramental religion, for ancient customs, and for ordinary decency in worship was so desperate that the Protestants almost succeeded. It is this which accounts for the occasional Protestant phrases in our formularies and for a "double" standard of practice. These things are there, not because Protestant ideals are in accord with the mind of the Church of England, but because it was necessary at times, in the desperate war for survival that was being waged, occasionally to turn a blind eye to the less important illegal practices of those who, in essential matters, accepted the position of the Church. In a war one accepts any allies. Only by the most determined vigilance were the Elizabethan bishops able to enforce a minimum of decency upon the Protestant extremists.[1]

5. *The Meaning of Words*

Words, invented to allow man to express his thoughts and therefore to share them with others, have been used also to clog thought, to befog controversy, and to bludgeon and batter opponents. Never was this more clear than in the Reformation period, when about half Western Christendom thundered against the other half, using the same word in a different sense. In the controversy about transubstantiation the Church of England

[1] For details about this consult Frere in *History of the English Church*, Vol. V.

protested against something which had never been officially taught, and was anathematized for holding something which it rejected. Since then, outside religious controversy, we have learnt that the first step in understanding any position is to discover what people mean by the words they use. We have seen also that one of the worst mistakes an historian can make is to use words as if they had meant years ago what they mean to-day. If the word "prevent", which occurs in the Elizabethan prayer book, was to be interpreted in the sense in which we use it, we should get something almost exactly the opposite of what was originally intended. For in Tudor times "prevent" meant something like "lead on", whereas to-day it means "stop".

Amongst terms whose meaning has changed and whose misuse has bedevilled controversy are "Romish", "Catholic", "Protestant", and "the Sacrifice of the Mass". Romish is dealt with sufficiently elsewhere.[1] A note about the other three may be useful at this point. They all occur constantly in modern controversies, and are used in ways which suggest that they meant for the Elizabethans what they mean to us. But they did not.

The Church in Tudor times drew a clear distinction between the "sacrifice of Masses" and the "sacrifice of the Mass". To ignore this is to be guilty of one of the sins to which popular historians are always liable. Thus a Jesuit pamphleteer has written lately, "the National Church went to extraordinary lengths to abolish the Mass. Men were killed for saying it, and men and women were persecuted for hearing it."[2] Neither of those sentences is true. There was no killing of priests who used the unreformed Latin service, and very little actual persecution of them or their congregations (though the written law provided penalties for those described as singing, saying, or hearing mass[3]), *until* the Pope declared war on Elizabeth. Frere says that until 1563 "the dealings had been exceedingly lenient; imprisonments were few, even the fines for non-attendance at church do not seem to have been levied."[4] It was a massacre of Protestants in France

---

[1] Chap. 15.   [2] Father J. Christie, S.J.
[3] Viz., the Statutes of 23 Eliz. I, c.1, 3 Jac. I, c.5 ; and 11 & 12 Will. III c.14.
4 *History of the English Church*, Vol. V.

which inaugurated stricter measures in England. The French government, by an edict in 1562, had removed all penalties attached to Huguenot worship, and less than three months later a number of Protestants were massacred at Vassy, while unarmed and engaged in worship. But in spite of the wrath which this aroused, there were still no executions until the Pope began to stir up foreign enemies to attack England. Then, and not till then, celebrating or assisting at the unreformed Mass became a serious crime, because those who did so were regarded as enemies of the country, and indeed, beyond question, some of them were. The argument that the Mass was abolished because the Latin Mass was prohibited can be sustained only if the reformed service was not a true Mass. As will be shown in its proper place,[1] this can only be maintained if the English rite is not examined. If it is given anything like just consideration it will be seen that, although the English Church protested against the "sacrifice of Masses", it carefully preserved the "sacrifice of the Mass".[2]

Roman Catholic enemies of the Church of England have lately revived also the stupid argument that the Church of England is a Protestant body, because Elizabeth and her loyal subjects commonly described themselves as Protestants. They did. Nevertheless the argument is stupid because it attributes to the term the meaning which it has acquired to-day. It ought to be obvious that when Churchmen to-day call themselves Catholics they do not intend to imply that they are Papists. Indeed to distinguish themselves from such they often use the prefix "Anglo-". In the Elizabethan days Protestant was the opposite of Papist, so that when men called themselves Protestants they did not mean that they were not Catholics, but that they were not Papists. To Anglicans of that period, and to the Easterns, Papism and Catholicism were wholly incompatible. All Easterns and Anglicans are Protestant, because they protest against the claims which the Papacy makes to universal jurisdiction and infallibility. These claims are uncatholic. Because that was believed to be true, Elizabeth was proud to call herself a Protestant, and by doing so she thought that she laid claim to the title of Catholic. As a matter of fact she frequently called herself one. She was gravely offended,

[1] Chap. 12.   [2] Ibid.

because the Pope did not consult her before summoning the Council of Trent, as he did the other Catholic sovereigns, and this was one of the reasons why the English bishops were absent from that council. When she protested to the Spanish ambassador about this slight, she told him that she was "as Catholic as any in the kingdom",[1] including himself.

The attempt to lump the Church of England amongst the Protestant connections by giving to controversial terms unhistoric meanings is no new one. Its underlying assumption is that Rome is the whole Catholic Church, and that therefore whatever Rome does must be Catholic and right. To depart in any way from Roman faith, or custom, must be a sign of heretical opinion, or schismatical practice. It must be uncatholic. This curious attitude, which ignores the unchanging East, is as old as the Reformation. As early as 1563, Bishop Pilkington, answering a Roman libel that the Church of England had declined from the old Church, said "under the name of Church he ever understands Rome".[2]

6. The Policy of Persecution

In recent years a very great deal has been written and spoken, monstrously unjustly, about the Elizabethan policy of persecution. It is true, of course, that many of the men and women who suffered in her reign believed that they died for their faith. That conviction, coupled with their shining courage, may justify their being regarded as martyrs, although it has always been considered that the title belonged rightly only to those who died for the true faith. Roman Catholics declare that this is exactly what they did. Those of us who believe that assertion to be false can still pay them the tribute due to all men and women who hold steadfastly to what they accept as true, whatever the cost.

Very few, if any, religious persecutions have been purely religious. Christians in the classical empire struggled for freedom of conscience and worship, but were persecuted as dangerous to the State. In all the conflicts of the Reformation period, and in every country, one aim always was the overthrow of the *de facto*

[1] Frere, *History of the English Church*, Vol. V.
[2] Pilkington, *Confutation*.

government. In England both Papists and Puritans had their own programmes, political, as well as religious.

When to an internal struggle for power there is added a threat of foreign attack, a government is faced with the peril which we have learnt to call "the fifth column". This greatly increases the strain and, unless very firmly handled, it can produce national hysteria. We have not forgotten German spy and invasion scares. But on the whole, Reformation England, the England of Elizabeth, was singularly well controlled and sane. The country had been sickened by the fires of Mary's reign and yet there was nothing in the nature of retaliation. Until the Pope declared war on the Queen, Papists were allowed to live in peace, and many of them held positions of authority at Court and throughout the country. Mary had martyred five bishops, but no Marian bishop suffered death. Consider these dates:

Elizabeth succeeds to the throne	1558
Mary of Scotland enters England	1568
The Northern Rebellion in favour of Mary, subsidized by the Pope	1569
Bull of excommunication declaring Elizabeth a usurper	1570
Ridolfi plot against Elizabeth	1571
Massacre of St Bartholomew	1572
Invasion of Ireland, directed by a papal envoy	1579
Throgmorton's plot against Elizabeth	1583
Babington's plot against Elizabeth	1584
Execution of Mary of Scotland	1587
Spanish Armada sails with papal blessing	1588

There were in England all the conditions which might have led to hysteria. But although nonconforming Papists were fined, no one died for his religion during the first ten years of Elizabeth's reign, and that in spite of the fact that the death sentence was pronounced with terrible frequency in all courts of law. A. L. Rowse says that for ordinary civil and criminal offences there were 74 persons hanged in one county alone in a single year. But religious executions do not begin until after the arrival of Mary, Queen of Scots. When they do, only the most prejudiced against Elizabeth's government could salute many of the sufferers as martyrs. The Earl of Northumberland, who played a prominent part in the Northern rebellion in favour of the Scottish Queen, has been beatified by Rome, but he actually took up arms against the Queen to whom he had sworn fidelity. Even after the plots against the Queen's life had begun the government acted with extraordinary leniency, preferring in most cases to exile, rather than to execute. This is truly remarkable, when viewed in connection with the hardness of the age, the political dangers of the government, and the violence of the contemporary religious prejudice. No member of the government has been more consistently held up to execration than Walsingham. He has been called the head of the Elizabethan gestapo, and his methods have been constantly vilified. But as a matter of fact he was a consistent Protestant. He had gone into exile in Mary's reign and was English ambassador in Paris on the night of the Massacre of St Bartholomew, when he sheltered many Huguenots in his home and saved them from death. Is it surprising that a convinced Protestant, with vivid personal memories of that night of terror, should have been an implacable enemy of Papists? But even he never let his feelings completely swamp his sense of justice. All the government ever sought was outward conformity. There never was anything in England corresponding to the Inquisition, which inquired into men's inmost faith. Again and again Elizabeth declared that what men believed in their hearts was a question with which she had no concern. She wanted loyalty and valued conformity as proof of it. Roman Catholics have waxed eloquent about what they call the "Bloody Question", which was put to recusants, and was the nearest approach to an inquisition of conscience. It was "do you believe that the Pope has a right to dispense from oaths of fidelity to the sovereign?" But after the Pope, who claimed this right, had declared war, and had subsidized rebels, was it an unfair test? And was it not a political, rather than a religious, test? Prisoners claimed that they suffered for religion and were loyal to the Queen. But the Pope had declared that Queen a usurper, absolved all her subjects from oaths of loyalty, and forbidden them to obey her, under pain of excommunication. (The text of the Bull will be found on page 191.) How could the government trust protestations of loyalty made by men who believed that God's vicar had absolved them from breaches of their oaths of obedience? Rowse declares that "One could draw a graph of the number of executions showing how they go up and down with the crises of the times, increasing from 2 in 1583 to 15 in 1584, the threshold of war, reaching their apogee in 1588 (the year of the Armada) with a holocaust of 34 victims. With the comparative security of 1589 the number falls to 9",[1] and continues to decline until it reaches 1 in 1603. What do all the executions for religion and politics add up to for the 44 years of Elizabeth's reign? One hundred and twenty-four priests and 63 lay men and women, that is 187 martyrs in all. Terrible? Yes, but compare those numbers with some others of the period.

In Mary's reign of 4 years there were 288 executions. Does not Elizabeth's 187 in 44 years compare favourably with this?

The number of Huguenots who perished in the Massacre of St Bartholomew is disputed. But Hardwicke says that "there fell in Paris, according to the most moderate calculation, 2000 Protestants, and in France at large as many as 20,000".

Tout states that Alva boasted that he had killed in 6 years 18,600 Protestants. Very many more died in Spain before the Inquisition succeeded in burning out opposition.

But in spite of everything, fear, panic, internal treachery, national danger, religious prejudice, and bigotry, retaliation for suffering inflicted in Mary's reign—in spite of everything—the number of victims who suffered for their faith under Elizabeth was very small indeed, judged by contemporary standards, even if all who died for political offences are awarded the palm of martyrdom. Neither were the tortures sometimes used, nor the death by hanging, drawing, and quartering, hideously barbaric and cruel though they were, remarkably worse than other customary methods of satisfying "justice". To be hanged, drawn, and quartered could not have been much more painful than being burned alive, and it was certainly more speedy.

It is more than time that arguments based upon the cruelty of Cecil, the cunning of Walsingham, and the wickedness of Elizabeth, were consigned to the oblivion that is their due. Sentimental pictures of the old Queen, terrified by her conscience and by fear

[1] *The England of Elizabeth.*

of judgement, fighting off death, may have a grain of truth in them. No one can want to canonize Elizabeth. But in comparison with her contemporary rulers, with Catherine of France and Philip of Spain, she appears almost an angel of light; and who, in their senses, would have exchanged her servants Cecil and Walsingham and Leicester for Alva, Torquemada, and Guise? It is possible to state a case for cruel persecution against the government of Elizabeth only by ignoring the facts in the interest of a ridiculous sentimentality. All persecution is wicked and unchristian, and Catholic coercion of Protestants is as evil as Protestant coercion of Catholics, no more and no less. If this wickedness is to be measured at all, and blame allotted, then the only possible way to do it is by estimating which side inflicted the greater amount of suffering and cruelty. By that investigation the 44 years of Elizabeth's reign, during which the Church of England was consolidated in its non-papal phase, has by far the best record of any government of the period. That fact cannot be controverted by appeals to emotion.

7. The Elizabethan Settlement

We turn now to the consideration of the situation with regard to the great majority of the nation. The sixteenth century in England was not a deeply religious one. There was some enthusiasm, amounting at times to fanaticism, in small minority groups, but on the whole it was a materialistic age, one in which the standard of living rose rapidly. Its spirit was expressed in domestic architecture, not in ecclesiastical, and great men commissioned artists to paint pictures of themselves and their families to hang in their homes, rather than of saints, with which to adorn churches. It was also an age of immense intellectual and literary activity. The excitement and adventure of life were overflowing on all sides the channels in which thought and expression had been confined for centuries. There was so much to do, to think about and discuss, that was new in the material world, that men for the most part had little time or inclination for real spiritual adventure, although few, if any, questioned the fundamental truths of religion. What men desired was that things in the Church should go on in the accustomed ways, so that they should not be distracted from the pursuits of ends which really thrilled them.

In this Elizabeth and her advisers were at one with the great majority of the nation. They did not want a new Church. The reforms of Edward VI had been very unpopular, as the immense enthusiasm with which Mary had been welcomed proves very clearly. But Mary's efforts to stamp out heresy had frightened and alienated many. When therefore Elizabeth came to the throne, there was almost solid support for an anti-Spanish and anti-papal policy, and there was a much larger majority of people in favour of moderate reforms than there had been in the days of Edward VI. It was the needs of this great body of moderate opinion that Elizabeth and her bishops set out to satisfy. Their aim is frankly stated in the preface to the Prayer Book. They succeeded in their object in so far as they held the nation together until, as the reign grew to its close, there had arisen a genuine enthusiasm and love for the reformed system and great apologists, such as Jewel, Hooker, and Andrewes, had begun to come forward to defend its principles. These can be summed up in the phrase "Catholicism without the Pope". The reason why the vast majority of the nation at first tolerated, and then became deeply attached to, the Church of England, as it was transformed under Elizabeth, was because it was seen to be, not a new body, for example, such as the Scottish and Swiss communions, but the old continuing Catholic Church. Because it was that, Catholics could adhere to it, however much they may have missed some of the moving ceremonies of the medieval period. Elizabeth could not help losing the Papists, who thought her an illegitimate usurper. But she was determined to keep the great majority of her nation united and loyal. That meant that she could have no truck with Protestant fanatics, even if she had not detested them. She desired to be as tolerant as she could, but she was firm in suppressing extremes which, for any reason, threatened the stability of her government, or the liberty of her realm. She tried to win the support of the great majority of her subjects by as conservative a presentation of religion as was possible, in the face of the pressure put upon her from the Papist right and the Protestant left.

The Queen succeeded. In most places the Church passed from

the old to the new régime without much difficulty. The one outstanding change was the use of the vernacular. It is true that Protestant mobs destroyed much that was lovely of carved work and painted glass. In this, however, they acted not with the law, but against it.[1] The machinery of the Church continued to function in the accustomed way. Bishops were nominated, elected, and consecrated in accordance with long established custom. Now, however, they were resident in their dioceses, as they seldom had been in the Middle Ages. The fact that the archbishop did not receive the pallium from the Pope could have affected few. Every parish had its priest, most of them ordained in days before the troubles became acute. The fact that the priest, or bishop, now had a legal wife could have been no great matter, because for centuries very many of them had married clandestinely. The Catholic sacraments were still administered. Children were baptized as before, and confirmation was probably administered more frequently than in the Middle Ages. Absolution was granted, couples were married, the sick were visited, and the dead were buried. It must have seemed very much the same, except for the fact that a man could now understand easily what the priest said. The whole life of the Church moved along the old familiar lines and the mass of the nation rejoiced that it was so. For most people it *was* the old Church, and that is why the Protestants attacked it so bitterly.

What did Elizabeth achieve? The maximum amount of unity for the English people that could be combined with a far greater amount of liberty of opinion than was possible anywhere else at all in that period. On both extremes there were fools (or knaves) arguing for their own ideas of religion. Elizabeth made it clear that she did not wish to interfere with men's inner convictions. She had no Inquisition to inquire into men's consciences. A greater unity was achieved in Spain and Italy. But at what a cost! There was no liberty of thought at all: the Inquisition burned out all dissent.

It is only against the historical background of the difficulties which faced the government at home and abroad that anything like a just verdict can be passed on the Reformation in England. We can now turn to the consideration of the details of the things which, as a matter of fact, our religious leaders did.

[1] Cf. page 27.

CHAPTER 3

DOCTRINE ABOUT "THE CHURCH"

ON THE CONTINENT reformers for the most part abandoned the ancient conception of the Church as a visible body. In England this was not the case. Here it remained the Body of Christ, linked up through the apostolic succession of the bishops with the apostles and with our Lord, who commissioned them. In the collect for SS. Simon and Jude, which is a new one, not a chance survivor of the old order, it is stated that God himself has "built his Church upon the foundation of the Apostles and Prophets, Jesus Christ himself being the head corner-stone".[1] God himself had "knit together his elect in one communion and fellowship in the mystical body of his Son".[2] It is into that Church and communion that the children of the Church of England are baptized: "We receive this child into the Congregation of Christ's flock".[3] The Church into which they are baptized is the "ark of Christ".[4] There is still "one flock and one Shepherd". Men are not to be made some kind of new ministers of a new Church of England; they are still ordained to be "priests".[5] The faithful were still to profess their faith in the "One, Holy, Catholic and Apostolic Church". After communion they were to be assured that they were "very members incorporate in the mystical body"[6] of God's Son which is "the blessed company of all faithful people". That phrase "all faithful people" does not mean "Christians in general". It means people who "hold The Faith". In the prayer for All Sorts and Conditions of Men this is made explicit, for in it prayer is made that all who profess to be Christians (but are not of Christ's flock) "may be led into the way of truth". So also in a collect for Good Friday, where it is prayed that heretics may be brought home to Christ's flock, that there may be one fold under one Shepherd.

[1] Collect for SS. Simon and Jude.
[2] Collect for All Saints' Day.
[3] Baptismal Service.
[4] Ibid.
[5] Ordination of Priests.
[6] Prayer of Thanksgiving.

This Church of Christ is in existence, and the members of the Church of England are continuing members of it. The reformers are doing certain things about its worship and ceremonies but clearly they do not consider that they are making a new body. This is very clearly expressed on the title-page of the Prayer Book. The printers, in the interests of a well displayed page, have done a great deal to obscure the meaning, but it is obvious for those who will think. It runs "The Book of Common Prayer and administration of the sacraments and other rites and ceremonies of the Church, according to the use of the Church of England". Put into less technical language, this means that the Prayer Book contains the Divine Office, as Cranmer indeed called it, the Service of Holy Communion, the sacraments, and other rites such as the Visitation of the sick, and the Litany, of the whole Catholic Church, done in the way of the Church of England. The point is that all the sacraments, rites, and ceremonies are not thought about as being "Church of England". They belong to the whole Church of Christ. At the Reformation the Protestant communions abandoned bishops and priests; they ceased to have authorized liturgies; they made of the sacraments something new. But the Church of England is continuing to do the old things. The Prayer Book is a service book of "The Church".

But those old things are now to be done "according to the use [or custom] of the Church of England". This was a comparatively new principle. Before the Reformation almost every diocese, everywhere, had its own "use". There was then, as there is now, a very great diversity of custom between the West and the East. No one doubted that the things which were done in the Oriental rites were Catholic, although Easterns did them in their very different ways. So also in the West. In Paris and Milan, in Seville, Lyons, Venice, and many other places there were local uses. Even the use of Rome itself was local. Traces of many of these uses have survived to the present day. One of the aims of the reformers was to replace all diocesan uses by a national one. "And whereas there hath been great diversity in saying and singing in Churches within the Realm; some following Salisbury Use, some Hereford Use, and some the Use of Bangor, some of York, some of Lincoln; now, from henceforth all the whole Realm shall have but one

3

Use."[1] It is a fact, of course, that this goal was never reached and that, probably, we have in our churches to-day far greater diversity than existed before the Reformation. But uniformity was something which the reformers set out to attain. It was a completely Catholic aim and indeed anticipated the same kind of movement by Rome. In itself it need not have caused any breach of unity, for there was nothing reprehensible in the principle.

In carrying out this ideal of a uniformity of use for all the dioceses of the kingdom, differences developed between ancient and modern customs, and between those of England and the Continent. It is these differences that we have to consider. They were not intended to cause any breach of unity either with the past, or with the rest of the Church. But our reformers believed that they had the right to order things in an English way. They did not blame the Churches of the Continent for not following their example. "In these our doings we condemn no other nations, nor proscribe anything but to our own people only: For we think it convenient that every Country should use such Ceremonies, as they shall think best to the setting forth of God's honour and glory."[2]

The Church of England, in intention, continued to do the old things, its worship is the old worship, its sacraments and other rites are those of the universal Church, but the whole paraphernalia of worship was simplified. Into the details of this we shall inquire at the appropriate times. Here it is enough to try to make the point that in desiring a greater simplicity the reformers were well within the Catholic tradition. The Benedictine movement, the Cistercian reform, the Trappist reform, and the Roman Liturgical movement to-day, have all been marked by a return to greater simplicity. The preface "Of Ceremonies" states the case for this quite fairly. The reformers may have gone too far. They may have thrown away some things that were both beautiful and useful. But that there was real need for simplification was a fact, acknowledged by Rome. Although we may regret that such traditional ceremonies as those of Ash Wednesday and Palm Sunday ceased for a time, although we may admit that the complete abandonment of anti-

[1] Preface "Of Ceremonies" (1549). Cf. also the title-page of the Prayer Book.
[2] Ibid.

phons and responds in the Divine office, and the variable introits, graduals, communions, and postcommunions in the Mass, was a very great mistake, nevertheless these and similar actions were not outside the competence of two provinces of the Catholic Church. In no way do they, or can they, affect the questions of continuity or validity. The ancient custom of the Church allowed a very great liberty to dioceses, in all such matters.

The whole question is summed up for us in Article XIX, "Of the Church". It begins "the visible Church" and thus comes down at once on the Catholic side of the controversy about the nature of the Church. It repudiates the Protestant opinion that the Church is invisible with its members known only to God. On the contrary, it is a visible body. The Article runs: "the visible Church of Christ is a congregation of faithful men, in the which the pure Word of God is preached, and the Sacraments be duly administered . . . in all those things that of necessity are requisite to the same."[1] That is a wholly Catholic definition. A body which is heretical, or in which the sacraments are administered by men who do not hold the commission of the Church duly received through the authorized channels, or where they are administered with insufficient "form", or not with the appointed "matter", is not a living part of the Church of Christ. Before the Reformation the Church of England was most certainly a part of that Church. Our reformers believed that it continued to be, for they were sure that nothing which they did was either heretical, or contrary to Catholic custom. They had no intention of making a schism, or of making any change which would be so revolutionary, or important, that they broke away from the historic Body of Christ. Roman Catholics argue that in fact they did so, but it is sheer wicked malice for the former to suggest that our reformers had this intention. They intended to continue the historic Church of England with all the marks and activities, and with the faith necessary to a body which remained a living part of the Church which our Lord founded. Whatever they may have actually accomplished, it is beyond argument that they believed in one, holy, Catholic and Apostolic Church, and they had no intention whatsoever of belonging to any other.

[1] Cf. Chap. 7.

CHAPTER 4

THE VERNACULAR

NO PRINCIPLE at all was involved when Latin services were replaced by English ones. There is no holy language, in which alone it is right to address God. Nevertheless, the reformers somewhat overplayed their hand when they declared that "it is a thing plainly repugnant to the Word of God, and the custom of the Primitive Church, to have public prayer in the church, or to minister the Sacraments, in a tongue not understanded of the people."[1] In our Lord's time the temple services and probably those of most of the synagogues of the Holy Land were conducted in Hebrew, which for centuries had been a dead language. Most Jews learnt some Hebrew—our Lord for example, quoted from two Hebrew psalms when he was hanging on the cross. The language of his daily life was Aramaic, but it is probable that he prayed in Hebrew and never took part in a service conducted in any other language.

As the Church spread to the Gentiles its language became Greek. The New Testament was written in Greek, and even in Rome for some four centuries the Church worshipped in Greek. Towards the end of the fourth century the right was claimed to use what had become the "vulgar tongue" and Rome changed to Latin from Greek. All the autonomous Churches of the East use their traditional languages and Rome insists that the Uniate churches, that is to say the schisms which have split off from the oriental churches in order to be in communion with the Papacy, shall continue to do so. Since all the great branches of the Church worship in their own chosen language, the Church of England in the sixteenth century had as much right to the use of English as the Church in Rome had to that of Latin in the fifth.

There are two sides to this question, but obviously there are some advantages in the use in worship of a language which the

[1] Article XXIV.

people understand. From time to time letters appear in Roman Catholic periodicals arguing that the conversion of England will be impossible until Latin is abandoned, and that its use accounts for much of the "leakage" to other communions. Priests of the *Mission de France* say Mass in French. "Nor is France the only Catholic country that has roused itself . . . the Austrian clergy . . . have chosen a vernacular liturgy as a bridge to reach lapsed and indifferent Catholics and so on to the de-Christianised masses beyond them."[1] The bishops of Austria have given permission for all baptisms, except for the exorcisms, all marriages, and all funerals to be conducted in German. Vespers and Compline may be said in French and German. In view of this contemporary movement towards the use of vernaculars it is obvious that the mere fact of translation could not have been an act of schism. The Church of England is quite clear that the main principle involved is that people should be able, in the words of St Paul, to worship "with the understanding". "Though it be appointed, that all things shall be read and sung in the church in the English tongue to the end that the Congregation may be therein edified; yet it is not meant, but that when men say Morning and Evening Prayer privately, they may say the same in any language that they themselves do understand."[2] In the opinion of the Church of England true devotion is advanced by the use of a language which is understood by the worshippers, and very many Roman Catholics agree.

[1] *The English Liturgist*, February 1948.
[2] First Note following Preface, "Concerning the Service of the Church".

CHAPTER 5

THE APPEARANCE OF CHURCHES

OUTWARD appearances are not in themselves very important, but unfortunately the iconoclasm of lawless men in the Reformation period has been used as an argument against the claim of the Church of England to be the continuing Catholic Church in our country. It is not advanced by serious controversialists, but it has often been pressed in a way which has great popular appeal. Father Hugh Benson, for example, in his quasi-historical novels has made great and telling use of it. If the established Church remained the old Church, and its religion the old religion, then why were stone altars broken up and replaced by wooden tables, images of our Lady and the saints destroyed, rood-screens torn down, stained-glass windows smashed? If all these, and similar acts of vandalism, had been done by authority they would not in very truth disprove the catholicity of the Church of England. For again and again in the long history of the Church serious men have reacted strongly against excessive ornamentation. There has usually been a strain of puritanism in every reform. The hermits of the Egyptian deserts, the Benedictines, the Cistercians, the Carthusians, the Franciscans all began with strongly marked preference for utter simplicity. For example, the Cistercians had bare altars, no images, plain glass windows, and unembroidered vestments made of the commonest cloth. Today the Benedictines of Bec have an undecorated, unfrontaled, High Altar, and place upon it only two tiny candles. The crucifix, which is compulsory in Roman Catholic churches, is a processional cross which they stand at Mass behind the altar. A good many English people would not find it easy to believe that their Church was truly a "Roman Catholic" one. The "Liturgical Movement", which is continually influencing more continental Churches, is reproducing the conditions at Bec, with even greater severity. There is nothing uncatholic in a dislike of elaboration and ornament. Therefore, even if the

Church of England had deliberately removed the accustomed "ornaments" it would not, by such an act, have placed itself outside the unity of the Catholic Church. But it did not remove them.

Our Churches were defaced and despoiled by lawless mobs of extremists, although in some cases they were incited by ecclesiastics, who ought to have known better. But the destruction from the time of Elizabeth was against the law. This was not so in the time of Henry VIII and Edward VI; some of the iconoclasm of their reigns had legal sanction. But as we have seen, the Church of England was absolved by the Pope under Mary for all that was done in the reigns of her father and her fanatical little brother.

Where is the law in these matters to be found? It is in the Ornaments Rubric, which is printed in every Prayer Book just before the beginning of Morning Prayer. It runs " . . . And the Chancels shall remain as they have done in times past. And here is it to be noted, that such Ornaments of the Church, and of the Ministers thereof at all times of their Ministration, shall be retained, and be in use, as were in this Church of *England* by the Authority of Parliament, in the Second Year of the Reign of King *Edward* the Sixth." That rule is incorporated in Elizabeth's Act of Uniformity of 1559, and its meaning is perfectly clear. All the Ornaments of the Church, altars, pyxes, aumbries, and tabernacles, crosses, roods, images, lights, fonts, holy water stoops, banners, thuribles and so on, which were in legal use in the second year of Edward VI, are still to be "in use". All the old medieval ornaments, which had escaped destruction, were to remain. The chancels, with their furnishings, were to remain "as in times past". So far as the clergy were concerned they were to continue to wear the vestments, which had been the traditional use of the Church for many centuries, for these were in legal use in the second year of King Edward VI.

It has sometimes been argued that what the rubric authorizes is the use of the First Prayer Book. But this cannot be the case. It refers to a time before the First Prayer Book was legalized, and almost a year before it became the legal use of the Church. The rubric therefore must enforce everything that was legal at the end of the reign of Henry VIII and at the beginning of that of Edward VI, before the legalization of the First Prayer Book. A glance at the dates will prove this.

Edward VI ascended the throne on 28 January 1547.
His second year ended 28 January 1549.
Parliament legalized the First Prayer Book 29 January 1549.
Parliament ordered it to "come into use" 9 June 1549.

By no stretch of imagination can things be said to be "*in use* by the authority of Parliament" four months before the date appointed for them to begin to be used. The curious indirect wording of this rubric, a typical example of Elizabeth's diplomatic method, is explained on page 183. The only changes in English religion, which had the "authority of Parliament" before the *third* year of Edward VI were the replacing of Papal by Royal supremacy, the order enforcing communion in both kinds (1 May 1547), and an English form for administering communion after Mass. Parliament sanctioned no other changes until it passed the Bill to legalize the use of the First Prayer Book in the third year of King Edward VI.

In order to provide for emergencies, the Act of Uniformity authorized the Queen to take "other order" if that should be necessary. It rapidly became necessary. Protestant mobs worked havoc in many places breaking down the carved work and destroying the beautiful contents of the churches. Vestments were cut up to make clothes for women. Some of the clergy, even of the bishops, had adopted extreme Protestant opinions. They refused to celebrate at the altars, and set up tables around which they sat for their commemoration of the Last Supper. They refused to wear vestments, and conducted the services of the Church in their everyday attire. Oddly enough, it seems to us, they refused to wear out of doors the gown and square cap of their Order and paraded about in ordinary secular clothes. When the law was being openly flouted it was necessary for some "other order" to be taken. But the Queen would not act herself. She remained in the background, for it was no part of her plan to incur unpopularity. Nevertheless something had to be done to procure order, or else lawless actions would have led to riots and riots to insurrection and perhaps civil war. The Queen solved her problem by goading on Archbishop Parker to act. She, not the Archbishop, had been authorized to take "other order", but she would not come into the open.[1] Behind the scenes she bullied him until he produced regulations which provided a compromise. In 1565, 1566, and 1575 he published "Advertisements". These ordered, as minimum requirements, surplices with hood and scarf at all services in parish churches, copes in cathedrals at Holy Communion, and the gown and square cap as "walking out" dress for all clergy. Even these modest regulations were bitterly opposed and the battle went on until the Restoration. The Advertisements, however, never became the law of the Church, for the Queen refused to give the royal assent to them and she refused also to sign the Canons, which incorporated them. It is nonsense to suggest, as has been done, that the Advertisements cancelled the Ornaments Rubric, for they never became law. It is worth noting that the Ornaments Rubric still embodies the law both of the State and of the Church. In spite of the most violent opposition by the Puritans, who pointed out that it involved the use of all the old "objects of superstition" of the unreformed Church, in 1662 Convocation insisted on its retention in the Prayer Book and Parliament legalized it. This would have superseded the Advertisements, even if they had ever been legal. Thus, in spite of sentimental accounts of the lawless destruction wrought by a minority of fanatics, the Church of England officially retained, and retains, in its churches the order and appearance of the unreformed Church and, except for some five months when the Second Prayer Book was in force at the end of the reign of Edward VI, it has always directed its clergy to wear the distinctive vestments of the Western Church.

Even if it had done neither of these things the Church of England would not on that account have broken with the Catholic Church. However beautiful, however desirable, however useful may be external things, such as images or robes, and ceremonies such as the use of incense, or reverences paid to altar, or holy name, outward things cannot be of sufficient importance to cause schism in the Body of Christ. Even if the Church of England had made

[1] The reason for this policy is considered in Chap. 20.

its buildings as empty and bare as the Swiss Calvinists made theirs the reformers would not, because of that alone, have severed their connection with the Catholic Church. Still less can the wanton destruction of lawless mobs have caused the Church of England to forfeit its birthright.

CHAPTER 6

THE DIVINE OFFICE AND KALENDAR

ONE of the arguments used to discredit the claim of the Church of England to be the continuing Catholic Church in our country is that, although it went on calling its ministers by the ancient names of bishop, priest, and deacon, yet it meant something entirely novel by them. The truth is that it used the terms in the accustomed way and the proof of this is that it commanded its clergy to do all the things which the various Orders of Ministry had done from the beginning. One of these things was the daily recital of the Divine Office. In itself this may seem a matter of minor importance. But it is something which quite definitely belongs to the tradition of the Catholic Church, and it is a practice which all the Protestant sects abandoned.

The Christian Church seems to have taken over from the Jews the idea of regular worship at dawn, at the third, sixth, and ninth hours (Roman chronology) and at sunset. To these, additional times of worship were added, until at last the Divine Office of the Church in the West was arranged in eight services: Vespers and Compline (for the ecclesiastical day began in the evening, as the Jewish day did); Nocturnes, or Mattins, said at about 3 o'clock in the morning; later in the morning Lauds, Prime (Mass), Terce, and Sext; in the early afternoon Nones. This daily round of worship became an obligation for the Western clergy, secular as well as monastic, centuries before the Reformation, and there was a parallel development in the East.

But even in monasteries the rule proved very hard to keep. Therefore from early days there was a tendency to modify the rule. Often Mattins was said last thing at night, before retiring to bed. The day Offices were grouped together around the Mass, Vespers and Compline were said together at some convenient time in the afternoon. Thus in practice the eight "hours" of worship became three, and sometimes two. So far as the laity was concerned.

there was never any obligation for them to take part in any of them, but the more devout often made a point of being present in church at Prime before Mass and at Vespers and Compline (when said together) in the afternoon. A few of the faithful, who were literate, and who could afford the great cost of written prayer books (of course a very small minority), read some of the offices privately.

The reformers saw that printing and translation gave them a great opportunity of making the Office profitable to all the faithful. They also saw that it would be foolish to expect that lay folk could be persuaded to visit their churches eight times a day, when that ideal had proved impossible for the secular clergy, and even monks had been compelled to combine some services. Therefore they accepted the *fait accompli*. They condensed the eight-fold scheme into Morning and Evening Prayer.

The problem was complicated by the fact that the original purpose of the recitation had been obscured with the passage of time. As the reformers complained,

these many years passed, this godly and decent order of the ancient Fathers hath been so altered, broken, and neglected, by planting in uncertain stories, and legends, with multitude of responds, verses, vain repetitions, commemorations and synodals; that commonly when any book of the Bible was begun, after three or four chapters were read out, all the rest were unread. . . . Moreover, the number and hardness of the rules called the Pie, and the manifold changings of the service, was the cause, that to turn the book only was so hard and intricate a matter, that many times there was more business to find out what should be read, than to read it when it was found out.[1]

That cry from the heart is echoed to-day by very many Roman Catholics and supplies some of the reasons why the reform of the Breviary is being undertaken.

Our reformers' solution of their problem was to return to the principles which had originally inspired the daily Office. They ordered that the Bible should be divided into daily lessons in such a way that the Old Testament should be read through, almost in entirety, once a year and the New Testament twice a year. The psalter was divided so that it should be read through once a month. All the non-scriptural lessons disappeared. Most of the variable

[1] Preface, "Concerning the Service of the Church".

parts of the services were abolished, but the "collects" were retained, together with "proper" psalms and lessons for certain of the greatest days in the Christian Year. Most of the collects were translations of the old, but a few were replaced with new ones, some of them amongst the best features in the new Book. No one who cares to compare, for example, the old collect for Advent Sunday with the new one will be likely to dispute this. Some of the best "fixed" collects were retained. The old canticles —Venite, Te Deum, Benedicite, Benedictus, Magnificat, and Nunc Dimittis were retained. The Apostles' Creed and that called "of St Athanasius", both of which had belonged to the Office in the West, were retained also.

The obligation to recite the Office remained unchanged. It was not made binding upon the laity, although it was hoped that now the services were in a language which they understood, more and more of the faithful would be attracted to them. For the clergy the ancient duty remained. The rubric governing this runs: "All Priests and Deacons are to say daily the Morning and Evening Prayer, either privately or openly, not being let by sickness, or some other urgent cause. And the Curate that ministereth in every Parish Church or Chapel, being at home, and not being otherwise reasonably hindered, shall say the same in the Parish Church or Chapel where he ministereth, and shall cause a bell to be tolled thereunto a convenient time before he begin, that the people may come to hear God's Word and to pray with him."[1] This means that the ancient obligation to recite the Divine Office was continued for the clergy, and that now the laity were to be encouraged to join with them in this work. The Church has always realized that worship must be public, as well as private, for "true worship cannot co-exist with that failure in humility which shrinks from being one of a crowd".[2] The daily Office, with its blending of many parts, has always been "Common Prayer", even when recited privately by a secular priest hurrying about to visit his parishioners. He has said it in union with all the faithful on earth and with those who have passed beyond the veil. It is the prayer of "Christ in his Church, or of the Church in Christ . . . not an

---

[1] Rubrics 2 and 3 after Preface, "Concerning the Service".
[2] Colin Dunlop, *Anglican Public Worship*.

individual prayer, but the prayer of the whole Body, the very stuff of what we prosaically call corporate worship".[1] It is this which the Church of England continued.

Let anyone who cares to do so ask the question: "In simplifying the Divine Office, and contracting its services from eight to two, did the Church of England make such a breach with the past that it ceased to be the Catholic Church of our country?" The core and heart of the Office is still, as it has always been, the regular reading of the Scriptures, the regular round of praise, contained in the psalter and canticles, and systematized prayer according to the custom of the Church for the varying seasons, and commemorations. All these things our reformers preserved.

It is worth while remembering that they were the only reformers who did. The Continental reformers wanted to cut themselves off from the historic Church and to make a new start according to the indications they believed they found in the New Testament. Therefore they abandoned the Divine Office altogether, and the Protestant sects have nothing even remotely resembling it. Our reformers attempted to reconstruct what they had inherited so as to make it possible for the laity, as well as the clergy, to use it, and for both to recite it with more real devotion.

Some may think that all this is much ado about nothing, for the real battle of the Church of England must be fought on very different ground. But the question of the Divine Office is more than a skirmish on the edge of the great fight. It has an important bearing on the case that the Church of England did not invent a new ministry, which it called by the old names. This book is written to prove that our Church thinks of the Episcopate and Priesthood in the same way that the Universal Church does. Its conception of their duties is completely orthodox. Amongst these is the recitation of the Divine Office. Not only is this obligation one which is laid upon the clergy of the Church of England, but the office which they are ordered to recite is the old Office of the Western Church, legitimately adapted by the reformers to the needs of the times in which they lived. They succeeded in continuing an ancient obligation of the Catholic priesthood, for our clergy are ordered, in the Prayer Book, to recite daily the Divine

---

[1] Colin Dunlop, *Anglican Public Worship.*

Office of the Western Church "according to the use of the Church of England".

The Kalendar

The continental reformers abandoned altogether the observance of the Church's year, although they magnified greatly what they called the Sabbath. Thus the observance not only of Saints' days but also such days as Christmas Day, Ash Wednesday, and Good Friday was abandoned. Nowhere was this "reform" carried through more drastically than in Scotland. King James VI, before he came south into a happier atmosphere, once said, "the Scottish Kirk is the sincerest kirk in the world", because it had abolished such relics of superstition as the observance of times and seasons and festivals. In most Protestant countries Christmas Day was replaced by the pagan New Year, and in Scotland it was made a criminal offence to keep the festival of our Lord's Nativity. The Church of England never even considered giving up the elaborate system of commemorating the principal events in the life of our Lord and his Saints, which from the beginning it had shared with the rest of the Catholic Church. It is true, of course, that many of the old ceremonies connected with the commemorations were abolished. Very many regret the loss of such things as the candles of Candlemass, the ashes of Ash Wednesday, the palms of Palm Sunday, the veneration of the Cross on Good Friday. But the really important fact is not that the ceremonies which emphasized the lessons were lost; it is that the commemorations themselves were retained. And they were not retained by Protestants.

Into the details of the changes made it is not necessary to go. It is enough to note that the *Sanctorale* was drastically revised. The complicated medieval classification of festivals into Greater Doubles, Doubles, Semi-Doubles, and the rest was replaced by a far more simple one. The Elizabethan Prayer Book contained almost the same list of Holy Days as our present one does. Out of these were selected twenty-nine days for which "proper" was provided, but no provision at all was made for commemorating the majority. This does not seem a very sensible proceeding, but when the bishops at the Savoy Conference were pressed to suppress altogether the Saints' days for which no provision was made they replied that the names were "left in the Kalendar, not that they should be kept as holy days, but they are useful for the preservation of their memories" and for secular purposes. It is a not unimportant detail that in the Tudor and Stuart period a Holy Day meant also a holiday; and in an agricultural community the number of holidays is a very important matter.[1]

The English compromise cannot be defended as wholly good. The Table of Feasts that are to be observed is far too long for the days listed in it to be regarded as "of obligation" in the modern sense. The "Table of Vigils, Fasts and Days of Abstinence" is even more impossible. It would have been wiser to have had far shorter lists "to be observed" and greatly increased lists "of devotion". "Proper" ought to have been provided on a very much more liberal scale. But it is easy to criticize. The important fact is that at a time when Protestants were denouncing the whole idea of the Church's year and more especially the observance of Saints' days as "foul idolatry and a filthy dreg of popery", the Church of England preserved a Catholic Kalendar. It made provision for the regular observance of the long established "seasons" and in the teeth of great opposition preserved the principle of commemorating the Saints. If it be desired to judge fairly what our reformers did, it is necessary to compare the Prayer Book Kalendar and the provision made in it for keeping the Feasts and Fasts of the Church, not only with the practice of Rome, but with the accomplishment of the Protestant sects. If that comparison is made no one will accuse the Church of England of having come down, in this matter, on the Protestant side.

[1] For the contents of the collects for Saints' Days see p. 115.

CHAPTER 7

THE SACRAMENTAL SYSTEM

THE TERM "sacrament" has a long history of development behind it. In the beginning the word "mystery" was used to denote what we now call sacrament, and it is still so used in the East. "Mystery" obviously has a wider application than to certain definite rites and ceremonies. So also had the word "sacrament". St Cyprian, for example, as late as 250, speaks of a sacred symbol, a sacred bond, and a sacred truth as all being "sacraments". It continued to be used in this general way until well into the Middle Ages. Thus St Bernard applies it to the rite of the Washing of the Feet on Maundy Thursday. But gradually there grew up a disposition to confine its use to the rites for which can be claimed the authority of the New Testament, and to speak of the "Sacraments of the Church" as limited in number. By the eleventh century that number was fixed at seven. These were (and are) Baptism, Confirmation, Penance, which would be better called Absolution, Holy Communion, Holy Orders, Holy Matrimony, and Unction of the sick. This limitation of numbers was accepted by all the great schoolmen and was authoritatively defined by the Councils of Florence and Trent. By the time of the Reformation, the teaching of the Universal Church, for the Orientals concurred, was that a sacrament was a rite instituted by our Lord, with an outward sign, through which grace was conferred. It was a channel of grace, not because of the worthiness of either the agent or the recipient, but because of the love and action of God. But there were certain conditions. Before anyone could be a valid minister of sacramental grace he had to be duly authorized, and he had to make use of form and matter, which our Lord ordained, and which signified the grace involved. There had to be a lawful Minister, right Form, and right Matter. To receive the full benefit of the sacraments the recipient had to have true faith and the appropriate desire. Since the purpose of each sacrament and the conditions for its validity are different they will all be considered in detail, separately. The Church of England carried on all this body of doctrine. It uses the term "sacrament" in the sense which it had come to assume, and it defined it in 1662 as "an outward and visible sign of an inward and spiritual grace given unto us, ordained by Christ himself".[1] Our Lord said that except men are baptized they cannot enter into his kingdom,[2] and that except they partake of his Body and Blood they have no life in them.[3] This must mean that these two sacraments are "necessary to salvation". But it is not recorded that he said that any others were. Moreover as our reformers insisted, the other sacraments had no outward sign which the gospels certify as of our Lord's own appointment. That is all that they maintained. They left us free to hold that the five minor sacramental rites are true sacraments. Bishop Gibson, commenting on Article XXV, "Of the Sacraments", says "it cannot be said that this expression ["commonly called sacraments"] discourages the application of the name to them, any more than the parallel form of expression in the Prayer Book 'The Nativity of our Lord . . . commonly called Christmas Day', discourages the use of the popular name for the festival."[4] Rome has never asserted that the outward sign of all the sacraments was ordained by Christ himself, nor has it asserted that all the sacraments are of equal importance. On the contrary, it has said, "If anyone shall say that these seven sacraments are equal to one another in such wise that one is not in any way more worthy than another; let him be anathema."[5] There is no contradiction between the Roman and Anglican definitions. The difference is due to the placing of the emphasis on different points. So far from denying the status of sacraments to those rightly called minor, because our Lord did not state that they were necessary to salvation, the Church of England has provided for them all, except unction of the sick. That all these rites convey grace is the teaching of the Prayer Book, and moreover they have their roots in the New Testament. We are certainly allowed to believe that the apostles, who we know administered them all, had the authority and teaching of our Lord for so doing.

[1] Church Catechism (1662).   [2] John 3.5.   [3] John 6.53.
[4] Gibson, *XXXIX Articles*.   [5] Trent Sess., VII, C.3.

The Prayer Book doctrine of the sacraments is unquestionably Catholic. Zwingli taught that they were no more than badges or tokens of Christian men's profession, and outward signs of fellowship. Lutherans and Calvinists stressed them as witnessing to God's redeeming love in the past, although sometimes they regarded them as witnesses to present blessings. Our Article XXV accepts all this. It states that they are: 1. Badges and tokens of Christian men's profession; 2. Certain sure witnesses of grace and God's will towards us. Then it goes on to add: 3. That they are also "effectual signs of grace", that is that they actually accomplish that which they signify. The term "effective sign" was the ordinary scholastic one. Luther only accepted it with very considerable qualifications. The other great reformers rejected it altogether. Our reformers use it quite naturally. For them the sacraments are not just pictures, but channels of grace. In the words of the Catechism they are outward and visible signs ordained by Christ himself, of inward and spiritual grace which is actually "given unto us". The outward sign is a true "pledge", or proof, of the reception of the unseen, but promised, spiritual gift. As Bishop Forbes put it "they not only signify, they convey". In their formularies our reformers advance deliberately from the partial truth of Protestants to the full Catholic position.

With regard to the requisite Minister, Matter, and Form our reformers were equally satisfactory from the Catholic point of view. They preserved to each order of the ministry its accustomed duties and privileges, and laid it down in the Preface to the Ordinal that "no man shall be accounted or taken to be a lawful Bishop, Priest, or Deacon in the Church of England, or suffered to execute any of the said functions, except he ... hath had ... Episcopal Consecration or Ordination". They firmly rejected the foolish Puritan idea that the validity of the sacraments depends upon the righteousness of the ministers, for this would mean that everyone would have to judge, not only the outward life of every officiant, but his mind and heart as well. All sins are not disclosed, and because the spiritual health of any man's soul can be known to God alone, the Puritan doctrine meant that there could be no certainty of the validity of any sacrament. Article XXVI rightly states "neither is the effect of Christ's ordinance taken away by . . . wickedness [of the minister], nor the grace of God's gifts diminished from such as by faith and rightly do receive the sacraments ministered unto them; which be effectual, because of Christ's institution and promise, although they be ministered by evil men."

It goes without saying that it is highly desirable that the Ministers of God's Word and Sacraments should lead holy and godly lives, but, so far as the validity of their acts goes, the one essential is that they should hold our Lord's commission, derived from those who have authority to bestow it.

There is one further point which calls for comment. Although Rome and the Prayer Book say what is fundamentally the same thing, the accent is somewhat different in each case. Throughout the Middle Ages the emphasis was placed on what the sacraments accomplish. But at the Reformation it was placed on how the sacraments ought to be received. In them God offers to us the grace which he promised and which is appropriate to each, but simply to receive the sacraments bodily is not enough. If we are to benefit by them we must receive them rightly—we must have right faith, true penitence, and a sincere desire to live as God wills we should. If we have not these dispositions the sacraments do not avail for our salvation. But when they are received in an honest and true heart they bring forth fruit unto eternal life, for their grace comes not from men but from Christ himself. In consequence "they have their effects when the receiver doth not put any bar against them".[1] This is the doctrine of the Church of England and it is good Catholic doctrine also, as St Thomas Aquinas bears witness. In all their sacramental teaching the reformers remained firmly on the side of the Catholic Church.

[1] The bishops at the Savoy Conference.

CHAPTER 8

HOLY ORDERS

THIS SACRAMENT is the crux of the whole controversy, and therefore it might be logical to consider it at the end of the argument. But since one of the points which our Roman antagonists make is that the Church of England did not intend to continue Holy Orders in the old Catholic sense, there are some advantages in facing the question early in the argument. If our case fails here it must fail everywhere. If therefore we consider what the reformers did about Holy Orders we shall be in a position to examine the functions of the ministry one by one as we consider the sacraments separately.

First our reformers were right in declaring that Holy Orders is not a sacrament in the sense in which they used that term. It has no outward sign which the gospels, or indeed the other writings of the New Testament, prove was "ordained of Christ", nor is it universally necessary to the salvation of every individual in the sense in which Baptism and Holy Communion are. But they certainly taught that it is a sacrament, in that it has an outward sign of at least apostolic appointment, and that through it there is bestowed the special gift of the Holy Spirit for the work of the ministry. The Orders of the Church of England have been condemned by Rome on the grounds of faulty intention and insufficient Ministers, Form, and Matter. The method which will be pursued here will be first to consider the history and doctrine of the ministry in general, and then to take the three great Orders in turn, searching the practice of the Church of England for evidence as to whether the Roman charges have any justification in fact.

The Authorized Ministry

The Catholic Church has always believed that our Lord bequeathed the fullness of his authority to his apostles. After his ascension they became, so to speak, his tongues and hands, the ambassadors, through whom he carried on his work of salvation. At different times he commissioned them to speak for him ("He that heareth you, heareth me")[1]; to forgive sins ("whosesoever sins ye remit, they are remitted")[2]; to judge ("whosesoever sins ye retain, they are retained")[3]; to graft new members on to his Body ("baptizing . . . in the name of the Father, and of the Son, and of the Holy Ghost")[4]; to celebrate Holy Communion ("This is my Body . . . this do in remembrance of me.").[5] From the Acts we learn that the apostles believed that they were authorized to "lay hands" in order to commission others to share in their ministry.[6] Their deeds show also that they believed they were authorized to lay hands in order that the Holy Spirit might be bestowed.[7] All these authorities were summed up in what might be called the consecration service, which took place in the Upper Room after the resurrection. "Then said Jesus to them again, Peace be unto you: As my Father hath sent me, even so send I you. And when he had said this, he breathed on them, and saith unto them, Receive ye the Holy Ghost."[8]

The view that our Lord appointed St Peter to be the Prince of the apostles and his Vicar, so that he became the channel through which our Lord's authority flowed to the other apostles, which Roman Catholics assert, but which the East and the Church of England deny, will be considered in Chapters 16 and 17. Apart from this point there is no controversy at all in the Catholic Church about our Lord's bestowal of authority upon his apostles. In the Acts and Epistles we find them claiming to be his representatives and exercising, by his command, his full authority.

As the numbers of men and women joining the Church were multiplied the apostles discovered that they needed helpers. Therefore they delegated part of their authority to others. They made seven deacons to take some of the burden of secular administration off their shoulders. There does not seem to have been any more doubt in their minds that they had the right to do this, than there was when they consecrated St Matthias to fill the place of Judas. If our Lord had come from the Father with authority to

[1] Luke 10.16.   [2] John 20.3.   [3] John 20.23.   [4] Matt. 28.19.
[5] Luke 22.19,20.   [6] Acts 13.3; 6.8.   [7] Acts 8.17.   [8] John 20.21,22.

send them, and if he sent them out into the world possessed of his authority, then they must have been acting within their commission when they sent others to do things which it was beyond their capacity to do themselves. Later we find them acting on this same principle when they laid hands on St Paul and St Barnabas, consecrating them to be in a special way apostles to the Gentiles. Later still, we read of the ordination of presbyters, or elders, in every city, that they might exercise authority in the Church during the absence of the apostles.

So far the facts are quite clear. It is not so clear how the ministry of apostles, presbyters, and deacons grew into the three-fold ministry with which we are familiar. There is a gap of about fifty years between the relevant statements in the books of the New Testament and the beginnings of history proper, and it is in this gap that the development took place. Were the elders (presbyters) mentioned in the Acts what we understand as bishops, or priests, or a combination of both? It seems certain that in the absence of the apostles they ministered to the Churches in the place of the apostles. For example, they must have celebrated the Eucharist. The first Epistle to the Corinthians proves that someone did so, in the absence of St Paul. But the apostles, who exercised what may be called a ."roving commission", supervised these local ministries. Even before the end of the period of direct apostolic control something like "presiding elders", or bishops, such as St Timothy and St Titus begin to appear. At the beginning of the second century these "overseers" of the local Churches are unmistakable. They may have arisen out of the body of presbyters by force of personal character, or by the wish of the other presbyters, or by the choice of the local Church. On the other hand it is more likely that they were appointed to the pre-eminence by the apostolic founder of the Church. St Paul writes to St Timothy and St Titus as if they possessed a peculiar "overseeing office", which they had received from him, and there is an unshakeable tradition that the apostles appointed St Ignatius and St Polycarp to be what we should call bishops. Here are a few revelant quotations from the Fathers.[1] St Clement (about 95) writes: "Christ is from God, and the apostles from Christ . . . and they appointed

[1] They can be found in Bettenson's *Documents of the Christian Church.*

their first-fruits to be bishops and deacons. . . . They appointed the aforesaid, and after a time made provision that on their death other approved men should succeed to their ministry." St Ignatius in the epistle to the Smyrnaeans, which he wrote on the way to martyrdom, about 112, said: "All of you follow the bishop as Jesus Christ followed the Father, and follow the presbyters as the apostles; and respect the deacons as the commandment of God. Let no man perform anything in the church without the bishop. Let that be considered a valid eucharist over which the bishop presides, or one to whom he commits it." St Irenaeus wrote (about 170): "The blessed apostles, after founding and building up the Church [in Rome] handed over to Linus the office of bishop. Paul mentions this Linus in his epistles to Timothy. He was succeeded by Anacletus, after whom, in the third place after the apostles, Clement was appointed bishop. He not only saw the blessed apostles but also conferred with them, and had their preaching ringing in his ears, and their tradition before his eyes." This is the St Clement, who is quoted above. About 198 Tertullian wrote of the apostolic succession as the test of orthodoxy: "Let them produce the origins of their churches; let them unroll the list of their bishops, an unbroken succession from the beginning, so that the first bishop had as his precursor, and the source of his authority, one of the apostles." It will be noted how universal this testimony is. It comes from Rome, Asia, Gaul, and Africa.

It is sometimes argued that this succession of which the Fathers speak was a succession in office, rather than a succession through consecrators. That may be true of the lists, but even so it is certain that no one ever succeeded to a bishopric save by consecration. The method of appointment has varied from popular clamour to nomination by Sovereign or Pope. But always the person designated has been no more than "bishop elect", until he has received the apostolic commission from men who were entitled to hand it on.

From this survey two things emerge as certain. First, there has always been in the Church an "authoritative" ministry, claiming to exercise the powers which our Lord bestowed upon his apostles, and secondly, that it is the firm tradition of the Church that the delegating of the powers of this ministry to bishops, priests, and deacons was the work of the apostles.

The Protestant sects all broke away completely from this tradition. They either dispensed with bishops, like the Presbyterians, or else they set up entirely new ministries for themselves, whose authority depended upon either some alleged inward and unproveable call from God, or else was derived from the congregations whom they served. What did the Church of England do? Pope Leo XIII declared, when he condemned Anglican Orders as invalid, that our reformers had had no intention of continuing the historic, apostolic ministry. Nothing could be more certain than that this judgement was false. Our reformers may not have succeeded in continuing the ministry of the old *Ecclesia Anglicana*—we shall deal with this when we consider the Orders separately. But that they intended to continue the ancient orders of the Church there is no possible doubt. They said so with the utmost clarity and they came down without hesitation on the Catholic side of the controversy. "It is evident to all men diligently reading holy Scripture and ancient Authors, that from the Apostles' time there have been these Orders of Ministers in Christ's Church; Bishops, Priests, and Deacons. . . .[1] And therefore, to the intent that these Orders may be continued . . . No man shall be accounted or taken to be a lawful Bishop, Priest, or Deacon in the Church of England, or suffered to execute any of the said functions, except . . . he hath had . . . Episcopal Consecration or Ordination."[2] That is an absolutely straightforward statement of principle and declaration of intention. To say in the face of that statement that the Church of England, at the time of the Reformation, intended to set up a new ministry on the Protestant pattern is not only insulting, it is foolish. But, say the Roman controversialists, the real intention was quite different from the declared one, and this is proved by the fact that the Catholic Ordinal was exchanged for one which was invalid. Passing over the fact that if our reformers did not really intend to continue the Catholic ministry it was unbelievably stupid to say they did at a time when their country badly needed the help of Protestants, whom such a

[1] It is true that the latter part of this quotation is from the wording of the Restoration times, but the Preface to the first English Ordinal amounts to the same thing on any natural interpretation.

[2] Preface to the Ordinal.

declaration must alienate, we note that they did declare verbally, as clearly and as satisfactorily as words could do, that their intention was to continue the old ministry of the Church. Let us now examine the services which they drew up to implement their declared intention. Are they valid?

The Episcopate

The Episcopate is the High Priesthood of the Church. The bishop succeeds to the fullness of the authority which our Lord entrusted to his apostles. That is the teaching of the universal Church. In the earliest ages the bishop was the normal administrator of all the sacraments. He presided at baptism and "confirmed" the newly made Christian. He was the normal celebrant of the Eucharist. He administered discipline; excommunicating, imposing penance, and absolving. He consecrated others to be bishops. He ordained to the priesthood and minor orders. He was the guardian of the tradition of his local Church and, with his brother bishops, he was the guaranteed channel of truth, through whom the Holy Spirit defined the faith.

In course of time the bishops took their presbyters into partnership. Thus St Ignatius calls the presbyters the "Council of God" surrounding the bishop and says that they are fitted to him as "strings to an harp". Gradually most of the episcopal functions were committed to them, as we shall see in greater detail when we examine the priesthood. But some things remained in the hands of the bishop. Presbyters and deacons might advise the bishops, as St Athanasius, while still a deacon, advised the Council of Nicea. But the decision, in matters of importance, was made by the bishops. They "ruled" their dioceses and the united episcopate ruled the Church. Confirmation and ordination were the right of the bishop, for even when priests were allowed to administer confirmation the oil which they used had been blessed by a bishop. Priests never acquired the rights of excommunication, or of restoring to communion and, although priests were entrusted with a general authority to hear confessions and to absolve, the absolution of some sins was "reserved" for the bishop. Priests taught and preached under licence from the bishop. However the situation arose it is certain that in the second century the whole apostolic authority was in the hands of the bishops and that the presbyters exercised a subordinate and delegated one. This was still the position at the time of the Reformation.

Happily, with regard to the Catholic doctrine of Minister, Matter, and Form there is no difficulty. Only a bishop, of course, can consecrate a bishop, for only someone who has been given authority can transmit it. As a precaution, and to make validity quite certain, from the earliest times it has been the custom for the consecrating bishop to be assisted by others. Matter and Form have varied greatly in different places and in different ages. But there is no need for us to examine ancient forms. No one denies the validity of Roman consecrations to-day, and therefore it will be sufficient to cite the present Roman rule. This was laid down by the Pope in a decree, already referred to, which was published in 1948.[1] He said: "Having invoked the divine light, by our supreme Apostolic Authority and certain knowledge we declare, and as far as is needed, we decree and enact: . . . in Episcopal Ordination, or Consecration, the Matter is the imposition of hands performed by the consecrating Bishop. The Form consists in the Preface of which these are essential and therefore required for validity. 'Confer on Thy Priest the highest dignity of Thy ministry and furnished with every honour, sanctify him with the dew of heavenly unction.'"

The Ordinal proves that our reformers left the whole doctrine of the episcopate unchanged, for they carefully preserved the essentials of Minister, Matter, and Form. In very many different ways they showed that the Church of England in consecrating a bishop was appointing a ruler of the Church, a guardian of the faith, a successor of the apostles. They ordered that the consecrator should be the archbishop (or some other bishop appointed for the occasion). They made it necessary that he should be assisted by at least two other bishops, for they ordered that the epistle should be read by one bishop, and the gospel by another, and that neither of them should be the consecrator. At the actual consecration they ordered that all the bishops present should join in the laying-on-of-hands. Throughout the service it is made clear that

[1] See Appendix A.

the office which is to be filled is that of the episcopate in the historic sense. Two alternative epistles and three alternative gospels are provided. One epistle contains St Paul's charge to St Timothy; the other is his account of his own ministry which includes the warning to his successors: "Take heed therefore unto yourselves, and to all the flock over which the Holy Ghost hath made you overseers, to feed the Church of God." The gospels relate the story of our Lord's command to St Peter to "feed my sheep"; the consecration of the apostles after the resurrection; the order to the apostles to "go and teach all nations, baptizing, teaching them to observe all things whatsoever I have commanded you: and lo, I am with you alway". Each of these passages of Scripture bears upon the delegation of authority by our Lord to, and through, the apostles. The Church of England declares that it is doing what the apostles did. They fasted and prayed "before they laid hands on Paul and Barnabas, and sent them forth. Let us therefore, following the example of our Saviour Christ and his Apostles, first fall to prayer, before we admit and send forth this person."[1] Prayer is made for "this thy servant now called to the work and ministry of a Bishop"[2] that he may "faithfully serve thee in this office . . . to the edifying and well-governing of thy Church".[3] Amongst other things, the bishop elect promises "with all faithful diligence, to banish and drive away all erroneous and strange doctrines"[4] and to be "faithful in ordaining, sending or laying hands on others". He is exhorted to "be the flock of Christ a shepherd . . . feed them . . . hold up the weak . . . Be so merciful that ye be not too remiss; so minister discipline that you forget not mercy".[5] All this is in keeping with the ancient conception of the bishop, who is the chief shepherd of his diocese, its teacher, its ruler, the administrator of its discipline and the ordainer of its clergy, through whom he distributes the sacraments to the faithful, when he does not do so himself personally. The conception of the office is completely Catholic. The requirement that the ministers must be bishops is carefully safeguarded. The Matter is the laying on of the hands of at least three bishops, and the Form is "Receive the Holy Ghost (for the office and work of a Bishop in the Church

---

[1] Consecration of a Bishop.   [2] Ibid.   [3] Ibid.
[4] Ibid.   [5] Ibid.

of God, now committed unto thee by the imposition of our hands)[1];
In the Name of the Father and of the Son and of the Holy Ghost.
Amen. And remember that thou stir up the grace of God which is
given thee by this imposition of our hands, for God hath not given
us the spirit of fear, but of power, and love, and soberness."[2]
The Matter is that which the Pope has laid down as essential, and
it is not possible to maintain that the Form which he has declared
to be the Roman one is in any respect more explicit than our
English one. Compare them and then read the declaration of
intention as it is in the Preface to the Ordinal—"to the intent that
these Orders be continued". Is there any reasonable doubt that
our reformers meant what they said and that the means whereby
they implemented their intention were adequate?

There is one further point which must be considered before
passing on to the next subject. It concerns a malicious libel, which
no respectable Roman Catholic scholar would dream of uttering
to-day, but which unscrupulous controversialists still use, when
dealing with people whom they think may be ignorant enough to
believe it. It is that the actual succession was broken in Elizabeth's
reign. The successions of all the English bishops run through
Archbishop Parker, who succeeded Cardinal Pole. If Parker was
not duly consecrated none of the English bishops can have inherited the authority of the apostles. A story, called the "Nag's
Head Fable" was invented. It was said that Parker was never
consecrated. He was merely handed the Queen's mandate ordering
him to do the work of the Archbishop of Canterbury, when he was
sitting with some friends in the Nag's Head tavern in Cheapside.
The facts are these: Parker was elected by the Chapter of Canterbury on 1 August 1559. The election was officially confirmed by
the Province and received the Royal Assent in due form, and
according to custom, on 9 December, in Bow Church, Cheapside.
The consecration took place in Lambeth Palace Chapel on 17

---

[1] The words in brackets were inserted in 1662. They were directed
against the Presbyterians, who believed that there was no essential
difference between a bishop and a priest. After the suppression of the
Church of England under the Commonwealth it found it necessary to
dissociate itself from the Presbyterian position and to affirm that Catholic
doctrine of the ministry, which it had always upheld.

[2] Consecration of a Bishop.

December. Almost as if it was realized that the occasion would be
the subject of malicious libels, extraordinary caution was taken at
every stage to ensure that no shadow of doubt might rest upon it.
Two full accounts of the service were written down. One was laid
up amongst the Lambeth records. The other was sent for preservation to Parker's college in Cambridge, Corpus Christi. Four
bishops were involved; the celebrant Barlow, who was the Bishop
of Bath and Wells, consecrated with the unreformed rite under
Henry VIII; Hodgkins, Bishop of Bedford, who also had been
consecrated with the Latin rite; Coverdale the Edwardian Bishop
of Exeter; Scory, Bishop of Rochester and elect of Chichester.
The record of the ceremony is unusually complete. It took place
early in the morning, between 5 and 6 o'clock. Parker entered the
chapel preceded by four taperers. The four bishops took their
places on the south side of the altar; the archbishop elect, in his
doctor's robes, on the north side. After a chaplain had read matins,
Scory preached the sermon. Then the bishops retired to vest for
the communion service and returned through the north door—
Barlow attended by Bullingham and Guest, two archdeacons, as
his deacon and subdeacon, all attired in copes. The writ of consecration was read by Dr Yale; the litany was sung by the choir.
After the gospel, Barlow was seated before the altar, and the other
bishops presented Parker to him. All the bishops laid their hands
upon him and all in turn repeated the form of consecration. All
the bishops, and some of the other people present, communicated.
To say that in this consecration there took place a physical break
in the apostolic succession, is malicious nonsense. The episcopal
"Order" was continued beyond doubt, provided the form used
was adequate, and, as has been shown, that form was more explicit
than the one which the Pope declares to be the Roman.

The Anglican succession reached another "bottle-neck" in the
time of Charles I. All the English bishops trace their succession
through Archbishop Laud. In him was united not only the
Anglican line, but the Italian also, through De Dominis, Archbishop of Spolato, who took refuge in England from ultramontane
persecution during the years 1614–21 and assisted at the consecration of English bishops in 1617. In recent years Old Catholic
bishops, the validity of whose Orders Rome accepts, have also

taken part in our consecrations, thus introducing another line of succession.

The Priesthood

Enough has been said already about the origins of the Catholic ministry, and we can begin the study of the priesthood by considering it as it was when our reformers were accused of having abandoned it in favour of a new form of ministry. At the time of the Reformation the priest was the delegate of the bishop, ordained by him to minister in his absence to his flock. He was given a limited charge of souls of whom the bishop was the chief shepherd. He had been authorized to baptize, to celebrate the Eucharist and give communion, to bless, to hear confessions and to absolve from all save a few "reserved" sins, to preach and to teach on his own priestly authority, but he could neither excommunicate, nor lift the ban of excommunication. He was always subject to the supervision and direction of the bishop, who authorized the forms he used and could check and discipline him for irregularities in his private life, in his conduct of the services of the Church, and in his teaching and doctrine. The service of ordination was a very intricate one. It contained so many "climaxes" that it was generally said that all a man could know with certainty was that at its beginning he was a deacon and at its end a priest. It was not possible to state at what point the change took place. There was, in fact, a great deal of controversy about this. Some believed that the essential Matter was the delivery of a chalice with the authorization to offer sacrifice. Others found it in an anointing of the hands. Others believed it was one of several layings-on of the bishop's hands. Roman controversialists have usually condemned the validity of Anglican Orders on the ground that it did not contain a delivery of the chalice and a grant of authority to offer sacrifice, and in consequence was defective in Form, Matter, and Intention. But the more the custom of the primitive Church became known the more absurd this theory appeared. It would have invalidated the ordinations of priests throughout the first thousand years of the Church's life, for it is now known that all ceremonies of the Roman rite, except the laying-on-of-hands, are medieval. For many centuries Rome used only a simple laying-on-of-hands and a Form which had no mention of sacrifice. But were St Gregory the Great and St Augustine not priests?

We may thank God that this controversy is now dead, killed by the Pope himself. The papal decree of 1948 laid it down that "the laying-on-of-hands are and always have been in themselves a sufficient and appropriate sign of the sacramental effects of Order", and that the Form which validates an ordination in the Roman rite is "Give we beseech Thee, almighty Father, to this thy servant the dignity of the Presbyterate: renew within him the spirit of holiness, that accepted by Thee, O God, he may hold the office worthily, and win a good report by the example of his life and conversation." The first point to notice about this decree is that it goes right back beyond the Middle Ages to the custom of the primitive Church. The Matter of the sacrament is that which the New Testament shows the apostles used. In fact the Pope now agrees with the findings of our reformers. The Matter of ordination is the laying-on-of-hands. In the Form all pretence that it is essential to refer explicitly to the offering of sacrifice has been totally abandoned. In the Christian tradition the words presbyter and *sacerdos* are almost interchangeable, but *sacerdos* was the title used by the priests of pagan Rome, and it carries with it a clearer implication of sacrifice than presbyter. But this term does not occur in the Pope's essential Form. In that, God is asked to bestow the dignity of the presbyterate, not that of the priesthood (*sacerdotium*).

Turning now to the Anglican Ordinal, the first thing which meets the eye is that it contains a service for the Ordination of a "Priest", not "Presbyter"; that is to say our reformers made use of the stronger term.[1] Over and over again it is emphasized that the candidates are to be admitted to the "Order of Priesthood". The epistle tells that our Lord himself gave various ministries "for the perfecting of the saints, for the work of the ministry, for the edifying [building up] of the Body of Christ". The gospel speaks of the men whom the sheep have for shepherds, and in an alternative one our Lord presents himself to us as the Good Shepherd. In the exhortation which follows the gospel, the lesson

[1] All the official Latin translations of the Ordinal have *Sacerdos*.

of these scriptures is driven home. "We exhort you . . . that you
have in remembrance, into how high a dignity, and to how weighty
an office and charge ye are called: that is to say, to be messengers,
watchmen, and stewards of the Lord; to teach and to premonish,
to feed and provide for the Lord's family; to seek for Christ's
sheep . . . that they may be saved through Christ for ever."[1] The
actual Form of the rite is as follows: "'Receive the Holy Ghost
(for the office and work of a Priest in the Church of God, now
committed unto thee by the imposition of our hands[2]). Whose
sins thou dost forgive, they are forgiven; and whose sins thou dost
retain, they are retained. And be thou a faithful dispenser of the
Word of God and of his holy Sacraments: In the Name of the
Father and of the Son, and of the Holy Ghost, Amen.' Then the
Bishop shall deliver . . . the Bible into his hand, saying, 'Take
thou authority to preach the Word of God, and to minister the
Holy Sacraments in the Congregation, where thou shalt be lawfully appointed thereunto.'"[3] Compare this Form with that which
the Pope declares contains the essence of the ordination to the
priesthood in the Roman rite. Which is the more specific? Is it not
absurd to say that while the Roman Form makes a man a priest
the Anglican one is so indefinite that it does not? The office to
which the candidate is ordained is that of the priesthood, (*sacerdotium*, not presbyterate).[4] He is to administer the sacraments, which
obviously include Holy Communion. He is especially authorized
to pronounce absolution and he is given authority to teach. The
services of the Prayer Book show that he is to do all the things
which the priest is accustomed to do in the Catholic Church—the
recitation of the Divine Office is made obligatory for him, he is to
baptize, prepare for confirmation, absolve, visit the sick, bury the
dead, solemnize marriages, preach, and bless in God's name. All
these points will be considered in the services concerned with them.

The minister of the sacrament of Orders is a bishop, and no
one else. "No one shall be accounted or taken to be a lawful . . .
Priest in the Church of England, or suffered to execute any of the
said functions . . . except he hath had . . . Episcopal Ordination."[5] That is very clear.

[1] Ordination of a Priest.   [2] See note on p. 49.
[3] Ordination of a Priest.   [4] Preface to the Ordinal.   [5] Ibid.

5

But is it not one of the functions of the priest to offer the sacrifice of the Lord's Body and Blood? Most certainly it is, and has been since the time when the bishops delegated that function to them. But it was not customary to mention the fact in the form of ordination until the Middle Ages, and the Pope's decree proves that it was not necessary either at the time of the Reformation, nor is it necessary to-day. The Anglican priest is authorized to celebrate Holy Communion, and if this is the Christian sacrifice then he is ordained to be a "sacrificing priest". What the Holy Communion of the Church of England really is will be considered in the chapter on the Blessed Sacrament.

For the present these are the facts. The Church of England at the Reformation declared that it had the "intention" of continuing the priesthood. It directed that a bishop, and a bishop only, should ordain a priest. It ordered that the matter should be the imposition of hands of the bishop (together with all the other priests taking part in the service). The form which it adopted was far more definite than the one which is authoritatively declared to be the essential Roman one. The Church of England ordered its priests to continue to do all the things which for very many centuries priests had been doing in the universal Church. In all this it came down without qualification on the Catholic side of the controversy which was then raging between Catholics and Protestants. To say, in the face of these facts, that the Church of England intended to break away from the Catholic Church and to form a new body is utterly ridiculous. If lawful Minister, ample Form and Matter can make a man a priest, then the Church of England, beyond all argument, has retained a valid priesthood.

The Diaconate

The story of the making of the first deacons is told in Acts 6. They were in the beginning assistants of the apostles, and their duty was to relieve the apostles of some of their more secular tasks. Later they stood in the same relation to the bishop, organizing for him the finances of the diocese and attending him while performing his liturgical duties. The first of these functions is still performed by the archdeacon, and on more ceremonious occasions the bishop is attended by "deacons of honour", although to-day these are usually in priest's Orders. When the bishops began to delegate their liturgical duties to priests, deacons began to assist them in the same way that they had assisted the bishops. They acquired the right to administer the chalice at communion, to sing the gospel, and to preach under the supervision of the parish priest. In the East the diaconate remained, what it seems to have been universally in the beginning, a life vocation. In the West it became a necessary step to ordination to the priesthood, although some have held that a man can be ordained priest without receiving deacon's Orders, because the higher grade includes the authorities of the lower. Only a bishop can make a deacon, and the papal decree of 1948 lays it down that the essential Matter is the laying-on-of-hands and that the Roman Form is "send forth upon him, we beseech Thee, O Lord, the Holy Spirit, by whom he may be strengthened by the sevenfold gifts of Thy grace to fulfil the works of Thy ministry".

In the Prayer Book rite the collect and alternative epistles all equate the deacons with "the like office and administration" to that which the apostles conferred upon the seven first deacons. It is stated that "it appertaineth to the Office of a deacon, in the church where he shall be appointed to serve, to assist the Priest in Divine Service, and especially when he ministereth the Holy Communion, and to help him in the distribution thereof . . . and to preach, if he be admitted thereto by the Bishop". These are the traditional duties of the deacon. Assistance at the administration of communion, which was lost when the Western Church withdrew the chalice from the laity, is restored to him. The Minister of the sacrament is the bishop. The Matter is the laying-on of the hands of the bishop. The Anglican Form is "Take thou authority to execute the Office of a Deacon in the Church of God committed unto thee; In the Name of the Father, and of the Son, and of the Holy Ghost. Amen. Take thou Authority to read the gospel in the Church of God, and to preach in the same, if thou be thereto licensed by the Bishop himself."[1] Minister, Matter, and Form all comply with the Pope's requirements, for the Form is at least as explicit as the Roman one.

[1] The Making of Deacons.

Conclusion

The services of the Anglican Ordinal, in accordance with the most ancient custom of the Church, were inserted into the Communion service, deacons being made after the epistle, priests ordained after the gospel, and bishops consecrated after the creed. The actual conferring of the Orders was prefaced, again in accordance with ancient custom, by the "examination" of the bishop (which provided a pattern for that of both priests and deacons), the Litany and the Veni Creator. Bearing in mind the fact that large sections of Christendom were breaking away deliberately from the Catholic Church, denying the fact of the apostolic succession, and therefore its necessity, abandoning episcopacy and the priesthood, can it be maintained that the Church of England followed their example? Our reformers expressed their intention of continuing the threefold ministry, provided three services for doing so, ascribed to each order the traditional duties, and conferred the grace to do so through the episcopate, with what the Pope declares is "the sole matter" and with forms of words "which unequivocally signify the sacramental effects".[1]

[1] The Decree of Pope Pius XII, 1948, on Holy Orders is translated in full in Appendix A, p. 194. The Latin of the Forms is contained in Appendix B, p. 198.

NOTE. The substance of this chapter, with a closer comparison of Roman and Anglican Forms and the Papal Decree, can be obtained in pamphlet form from the Church Union, 6 Hyde Park Gate, S.W.7. It is entitled *Anglican Orders and the Papal Decree of 1948*.

CHAPTER 9

HOLY BAPTISM

BAPTISM is the initiatory rite of the Catholic Church. About its
purpose and meaning, and about its essentials, there is hardly any
dispute. It is founded upon the clear statement of our Lord.
"Except a man be born of water and the Spirit he cannot enter
into the kingdom of God".[1] He commanded his apostles to "go . . .
teach all nations, baptizing them into the name of the Father and of
the Son and of the Holy Ghost".[2] The Acts show that from the
beginning baptism was the way in which men entered into the
fellowship of Christ.

Why was it established? What does it effect? The answers are
identical, whether given in the East or in the West. Human nature
is a fallen nature. Man was created "to be the image of God's
immortality".[3] Through union with his Creator he was intended
to share in the love, joy, peace, and beauty which are of the nature
of God. But in order to do so it was necessary to will what God
willed. Man was created in the image of God; that is to say, God
who is supreme personality, the great I AM, made man a person
also. Like his Creator he can say "I", and because he can say
"I" he can say "I will, I want". He can desire and strive after
things which he knows are contrary to the will of God. Having
that power, at the very begininning of his existence, he fell. He
did what he knew was forbidden and separated himself from God.
Human nature is a unity. It is an inheritance from the first man,
and from the beginning the taint of sin has been passed on from
generation to generation. In consequence, without grace "we
cannot but fall".[4]

The Son of God emptied himself of glory and came into the
world to give it a second start. He became the Son of Man, the
second Adam. He lived in unbroken, conscious union with his

[1] John 3.5.   [2] Matt. 28.19.
[3] Wisd. 2.23.   [4] Collect for Trinity XV.

57

Father and by his life and by his death he broke the entail of sin.
He instituted baptism so that we might share in his victory, in his
triumphant life. In the first place, therefore, baptism is a washing
away of sins, past and present. Through it we receive forgiveness
for the original inherited taint of our fallen nature, as well as for
any actual sins we may have consciously committed. St Paul is
the great exponent of its meaning. Our Lord, he taught "hath
broken down the middle wall of partition between God and man"[1]
and he is the Head of the new body of humanity. Union with him
turns fallen man into "a new creature"[2] and because of union
with him men can draw upon a new unspoiled inheritance. It is
by baptism that we are made one with Christ, so that we share in
his life and his holiness. Our Lord himself gave us this idea of
unity with himself, he said "I am the vine, ye are the branches.
He that abideth in me, and I in him, the same bringeth forth
much fruit."[3] By baptism, then, we are "grafted"[4] into Christ as
a branch is grafted into a tree, and in consequence we become
sharers of his life, the entail of original sin is broken. We die to
our old sinful human nature. It is "buried with Christ"[5] in the
waters of baptism. We rise from them "partakers of the divine
nature",[6] possessors of a new nature.

In the beginning the normal minister of baptism was the bishop,
but that this was not a universal rule the action of St Philip the
deacon, as recorded in the Acts, sufficiently proves. In course of
time many of the privileges of the episcopate were delegated to
the priesthood and the priest became the normal minister, both
in the East and West. Probably because of fear of infants dying
unbaptized, by the fifth-sixth centuries the accepted rule, at least
in the West, came to be that laymen and women, in cases of emergency, might administer the sacrament. The Matter is water. At
first the catechumen was totally immersed, and this is still the rule
in the East. But this never seems to have been regarded as absolutely essential. It would seem very improbable that the 3000 who
were baptized on the Day of Pentecost were immersed, or that St
Paul could have immersed the keeper and his family in the prison
of Philippi. Moreover many early illustrations of baptism, such

[1] Eph. 2.14.   [2] Gal. 6.15.   [3] John 15.5.
[4] Rom. 11.24.   [5] Rom. 6.4.   [6] 2 Pet. 1.4.

as those preserved in the catacombs, show the water being poured. It can be said, however, that in the mind of the Church baptism by immersion, which was the way practised by the Jews for making proselytes, has remained the normal method, although pouring has become usual in the West. A relic of immersion as the right way remains in the regulation that sufficient water must be poured to "run" on the skin. Sprinkling is invalid.

The Form is "I baptize thee in the Name of the Father, and of the Son, and of the Holy Ghost", which is now held, universally, to be essential.

No fault can be found with either the doctrine or the practice of the Prayer Book. It teaches that "all men are conceived and born in sin",[1] that is to say they inherit a fallen nature. "Original sin . . . is the fault and corruption of the Nature of every man, that naturally is engendered of the offspring of Adam; whereby man . . . is of his own nature inclined to evil."[2] This entail of sin is broken by baptism "whereby . . . they that receive Baptism rightly are grafted into the Church; the promises of forgiveness of sin, and of our adoption to be the sons of God by the Holy Ghost, are visibly signed and sealed".[3] The congregation is exhorted to pray that God will favourably receive the person to be baptized, "that he will embrace him with the arms of his mercy, that he will give unto him the blessing of eternal life and make him partaker of his everlasting kingdom".[4] After the baptism and reception into the Church, God is thanked because he has been pleased to "regenerate"[5] the newly baptized person with the Holy Spirit, to receive him as a child by adoption and to incorporate him into the Church. He is then besought that since the baptized is "dead to sin and living unto righteousness and being buried with Christ in his death"[6] he may be made "partaker of his resurrection".[7] The Catechism sums all this up when it declares that baptism conveys "a death unto sin and a new birth unto righteousness; for being by nature born in sin and the children of wrath, we are hereby made the children of grace".

The Minister of the sacrament in the Church of England is ordinarily a priest. But a deacon may baptize, and in cases of real

[1] Baptismal Service. [2] Article IX. [3] Article XXVII.
[4] Baptismal Service. [5] Ibid. [6] Ibid. [7] Ibid.

emergency any lay person may do so. In this matter our reformers simply carried on the tradition of the Western Church.

With regard to Form and Matter the reformers were equally orthodox. The Form is the Trinitarian one taken from St Matthew which is common to the whole Church. The Matter is water, in which the Prayer Book suggests that the normal thing is to immerse the person to be baptized, whether child or adult. "Then he shall dip it in the water."[1] But if the priest is certified that the person to be baptized is weak "it shall suffice to pour Water"[2] upon him. It is very important to notice this direction, because Roman Catholics have queried the validity of our baptisms on the ground that we sprinkle. The Prayer Book orders us to pour. All the points which are universally held to be necessary are to be found in the Book of Common Prayer.

In the course of ages a number of minor ceremonies became incorporated into the baptismal service. Chief amongst these were exorcisms of the devil, a breathing upon the face of the baptized, and anointings with spittle and salt, and a signing with the cross. Many Roman Catholics on the Continent have already, without authority, freed themselves from these.[3] They were, in the words of the Prayer Book, "dumb and dark ceremonies". Our reformers swept them all away, except the sign of the cross. The Puritans did all in their power to get the holy sign omitted also, and they took exception to the Catholic phraseology of the reformed rite. They hated everything which savoured of priestly pretension, but with that curious perversion that distinguished so many of their opinions, they tried very hard to obtain the total abolition of lay baptism. They wished the Minister to be empowered to refuse to baptize the children of unbelievers, or of notorious sinners. They desired that the parents should be free to decide whether there should be godparents. They hated the blessing of the water. Above all they loathed the teaching that forgiveness of sins and regeneration are actually accomplished by baptism. All these points were pressed with a violence of language which to-day is almost unbelievable. But although the government of England sorely needed the help of the Puritans in the struggle against the

---

[1] Baptismal Service.   [2] Ibid.
[3] Cf. *The English Liturgist*, Feb. 1948.

Catholic powers of the Continent, the Church never gave way. Indeed it had the support of the government in the stand which it made for Catholic doctrine and custom. Nothing could be more certain than that in all which appertains to the sacrament of Baptism our reformers did nothing which, by any flight of imagination, could be held to cut off the Church of England from its past or to wrench it away from the unity of the Catholic Church.

CHAPTER 10

CONFIRMATION

UNHAPPILY both the doctrine and practice of confirmation is far less simple than that of baptism. The complication starts in the New Testament. Our Lord said that it was not possible to enter the Kingdom of God except by being born again "of water and the Spirit".[1] His words imply two things—water baptism, which was a Jewish custom, and Spirit baptism and one result, regeneration. Later on we find our Lord commanding his apostles to baptize. The use of water would seem to be implied, but although he spoke frequently about the gift of the Holy Spirit there are no definite instructions about what the apostles are to do to secure it, or how they are to minister Spirit baptism. We read in the Acts of how the Holy Spirit more than once "fell" upon people, quite apart from any ministerial act, sometimes before water baptism, as in Acts 2 and 10. We are also told about water baptism, and about a "laying-on-of-hands" which is followed by a gift of the Holy Spirit. There are also references to an anointing and to a sealing. It is all very obscure, but on the whole it seems likely that the normal procedure was to administer water baptism to converts and then to lay hands on them, for the gift of the Holy Spirit. Acts 8 suggests that this last was the work of the apostles alone, for St Philip, the deacon, although he had baptized his converts, does not seem to have felt that he was competent to lay hands on them. St Peter and St John were sent from Jerusalem to do that. Whether this laying-on-of-hands included some ceremony of anointing or not we cannot say with certainty, but it is very likely that it did, for the Jews practised an anointing in conjunction with water baptism, when they received proselytes. Also in the second century a common alternative name for the laying-on-of-hands was "Sealing", which implies anointing, and very early the anointing seemed to be the most important part of the

[1] John 3.5.

62

whole rite. In Syria it came even to overshadow water baptism. Theophilus of Antioch (about 180) could write "We are called Christians because we are anointed with the oil of God".[1] We cannot point to any precise words of our Lord commanding the apostles either to lay hands, or to anoint, but confirmation in some form begins so early, and so uncontroversially, that it is difficult to believe that he did not give them some instructions in the matter. Thus the Epistle to the Hebrews lists teaching about baptism and laying-on-of-hands amongst "first principles",[2] about which his readers know so well that it is no more necessary to explain them than it is to explain the Resurrection, or the Last Judgement.

The whole position becomes clear in the second and third centuries. Baptism and confirmation, as we can now certainly call it, are two parts of one service, and confirmation includes both a laying-on-of-hands and an anointing.

The normal practice seems to have been as follows: the bishop presided over the whole service. The catechumen went down into the font and there received baptism by immersion. As the water closed over his head, in the words of St Paul, he died to his former sinful life and was buried with Christ. Who was the actual minister at this point we do not know with certainty. It may have been the bishop. More likely it was a deacon, or possibly the man just lowered himself into the mystic grave. It is possible that custom differed in different places. Coming up from the font the newly made Christian was wrapped in a white robe to signify that he was now clothed again with the righteousness of his Saviour. He was born again to newness of life. Sometimes the metaphor was changed. He came out of the Land of Bondage and passed through the Red Sea of Baptism into the freedom of the Promised Land. He was then confirmed by the bishop, who anointed him with oil marking him with the sign of the cross. By this sign the candidate was "sealed unto the day of redemption".[3] Probably there was also a formal laying-on-of-hands. There was one almost certainly in the West, for a relic of it survives in the Roman rite in the prayer immediately before the anointing, which is said by the

[1] Confirmation, in *Liturgy and Worship*, p. 450.
[2] Heb. 6.1,2.   [3] Eph. 4.30.

bishop with hands outstretched towards the candidates. But, whether there was, or was not, an actual laying-on-of-hands, the anointing involved a virtual one, for it caused contact with the hands of the officiant. Immediately after the confirmation the newly confirmed was given communion. To this whole service was attributed everything which we associate with both baptism and confirmation, but because it was one service no one inquired what was the effect of its several parts—what does the baptism do? What does the laying-on-of-hands do? What does the unction do? The candidate went to the service a heathen. He came away regenerate having received forgiveness of sins, having been made a new creature, "a member of Christ, a child of God and an inheritor of the kingdom of heaven",[1] a "temple of the Holy Ghost".[2] The minister of the whole ceremony was the bishop, for even if he delegated parts of it to subordinates, he was present and all acted by his authority.

As the Christian community increased churches were multiplied in the towns and began to be built in villages. It became impossible for the bishop to preside in person at them all, especially as the initiation ceremony normally took place only at Easter and Pentecost. Therefore it became the custom for him to delegate his authority to the parish priests, who soon became the usual ministers of baptism. This led to a difference between its administration in the East and in the West. In the East the one baptism-confirmation service was continued, the priest doing all that the bishop had been accustomed to do. He baptized and confirmed, anointing with oil, which the bishop had previously blessed. In the West the service became two. The priest administered baptism, but the confirmation, now a separate service, was deferred until a bishop should be available. In the East the ancient unity of the service was preserved, but for all practical purposes it ceased to be episcopal. In the West the unity was lost, but the part of the service which the New Testament shows was originally the prerogative of the apostles, was still retained by the episcopate, although sometimes the authority to confirm in the Eastern manner with episcopally consecrated oil was delegated to a priest.

Eventually this breaking up of one service into two set the West

[1] The Catechism.   [2] I Cor. 6.19.

a very difficult problem. It was clear that the whole grace of initiation was conferred by baptism followed by confirmation. But when the services are divided, is the grace divided? What grace is conferred by baptism alone? What grace is conferred by confirmation alone? The Church in the West came to teach that baptism made a man a Christian, and it became the custom to admit the baptized to communion before they had been confirmed. Confirmation became more and more neglected and not infrequently people who were good practising Catholics never received it at all. Even to-day that is not uncommon on the Continent. As confirmation became less important in actual fact, naturally it became less important in doctrine also. What did it mean? What grace did it add to that already received in baptism (and Holy Communion)? It became customary to teach that it conferred the "fullness" of the gift of the Holy Spirit. In some sense it must be true that the Holy Spirit is conferred in baptism, for the baptized are regenerate, new born, and the Holy Spirit is the "Giver of life", therefore he must be active in the new birth. Moreover, it is through his action that all the sacraments become effective. "Every virtue we possess is His alone." If, therefore, it is possible to become a full member of Christ, partaking of his divine nature in communion, and bringing forth the fruits of the Spirit without being confirmed, what is the use of that sacrament? The difficulty is a real one, and it led in the Middle Ages to a steady minimizing of confirmation, until St Thomas Aquinas, for example, could teach definitely that it was neither necessary to salvation, nor a necessary preliminary for the reception of Holy Orders.

This then was the position which faced our reformers. They accepted the doctrine of initiation which was held in the West, and they attributed to baptism alone the graces which properly belong to baptism-confirmation. But they looked with disfavour on the popular neglect of confirmation. They felt that this was wrong, and they turned to the New Testament for guidance. What they read was puzzling. Confirmation as they knew it was administered by the bishop dipping his thumb in holy oil and signing the candidate on the forehead. He then tapped lightly the cheek saying "peace be to thee". They found nothing which suggested this in the New Testament, for they did not understand references to sealing and unction. They did find in it an actual laying-on-of-hands and they noticed that it was performed by apostles alone. They found that this action was associated with a gift of the Holy Spirit. They seized on these points and insisted that the minister of the sacrament must be the bishop and no one else, for he alone had succeeded to the fullness of apostolic authority. The Matter they said must be that which the apostles used, laying-on-of-hands. Unction, they thought, must have been a ceremony which developed when the Church had begun to lose sight of the apostolic tradition. For the Form they composed a prayer asking for God's blessing and a daily increase in the Holy Spirit.

Their intention, which is clearly expressed in the Prayer Book, is certain. There is no nonsense about the meaning of the service being found in the candidates confirming their baptismal vows. The Renewal of Vows was not prefixed to the service until 1662. As a preparation for confirmation it is wholly suitable, as indeed is the customary singing of the Veni Creator, or some other hymn to the Holy Spirit. But the essence of the service is not to be found in the preparation for it. The meaning resides in its exclusive episcopal character, in the laying-on-of-hands, and in the Form "Defend, O Lord". It is also expressed in the prayers which immediately precede and follow the administration of the sacrament, in which God is asked to impart the fullness of the gifts of the Holy Spirit. Our reformers were faced with a very involved situation, and a development which seemed to have taken the Church far from the apostolic tradition. They did not attempt to make a new service, but to make an old one express more faithfully the meaning of what the Church had done in the beginning. This is shown by the fact that the order of the Prayer Book service, except for the omission of the unction, is almost identical with the old Sarum one.

But did the reformers, in truth, actually preserve confirmation? For example, did they not deny to it the title of "sacrament"? They did not. They said, with St Thomas Aquinas, that it is not necessary to salvation in the sense that baptism and holy communion are. On the other hand they equated it with those great "sacraments of the gospel" for they made it a necessary preliminary to communion. They restored the ancient sequence of baptism, confirmation, and communion, which the East had always retained and which had been the original Roman custom. Few would deny that the sequence which they had inherited, baptism, communion, and sometimes confirmation, was an abuse. Further they refused to allow it to be ministered by any save bishops. The Puritans seized on this point. In 1662 they argued that this actually put a higher value on confirmation than on communion, which any priest was competent to administer. If it was to be retained, and many of them desired its abolition, then, they thought, it ought to be administered by priests. The bishops replied, "confirmation is reserved to the bishops as of old, and our Church doth everywhere confess to conform to Catholic usages of primitive times."[1]

From all this it is perfectly clear that the Church of England continued to treat confirmation as one of the sacraments of the Church. It is not possible to produce a shred of evidence to support any accusation of "minimizing", or of uncatholic teaching. We may regret that they made the matter of the sacrament the bare laying-on-of-hands, instead of combining it with unction as was done in the "very godly order" of 1549. But they did try to bring order where clearly there was disorder. In their doctrine they were wholly orthodox from the standpoint of the Western Church. They taught that the sacrament conveyed the sevenfold gift of the Holy Spirit. They restored its episcopal character. They emphasized what they had reason to believe was regarded as its Matter in apostolic times. Was all this the action of men bent on forming a new Protestant sect? Or was it the legitimate attempt of a living part of the Catholic Church to set its own house in order, by returning to what they had every reason to think was the uncorrupted custom of a purer age than their own?

[1] The Savoy Conference.

CHAPTER 11

CONFESSION AND ABSOLUTION

THE SACRAMENT of Penance was "ordained by Christ himself". There is no controversy anywhere in the Catholic Church about that, although its administration and scope have varied. After his resurrection our Lord authorized his apostles to forgive sins. "As my Father hath sent me, even so send I you. And when he had said this, he breathed on them, and saith unto them, Receive ye the Holy Ghost: whosesoever sins ye remit, they are remitted unto them."[1] The action as well as the words are significant. The Jews believed that life resided in the breath, and our Lord, by an action which the apostles would have completely understood, was passing on his life and therefore his authority to his representatives. "As my Father hath sent me, even so send I you." The commission and bestowal of authority were as absolute as deeds and words could make them. Then, very significantly, our Lord selected the most controversial of the powers he had exercised and underlined it. "Whosesoever sins ye remit, they are remitted." This was included in the general commission. Why did our Lord emphasize it? Can we be wrong if we say that he knew that the power to forgive sins would be one which his ambassadors would be most afraid to claim and that, if they did claim it, would arouse the most resistance? During his ministry he often said "your sins are forgiven"[2] and when he did onlookers at once began to murmur that this was blasphemy: "Who can forgive sins, but God alone?"[3] Once he worked a miracle of healing in order to substantiate his claim. It was because of his human experience that, when he constituted his apostles his representatives on earth, he mentioned specifically that he was bestowing on them the authority to pronounce absolution. In the epistles there are instances of the exercise of this power, and the Church has never doubted that our Lord bestowed it. Although God forgives sins, just as he gives the

[1] John 20.21.   [2] Luke 5.20.   [3] Luke 5.21.

68

grace which flows through the other sacraments, when and how he wills, nevertheless there is an ordained way in which forgiveness is granted. That has been believed by the Church from the beginning. God had commanded his Ministers to bestow it upon those who are truly repentant.

What, then, did our reformers do about this doctrine and practice? They continued it unchanged, except for one particular. The system which they inherited laid it down as of obligation that every Christian should seek absolution, through confession, at least once a year and before communion. The reformers removed the compulsion and left it to each man to decide whether he had sinned in such a way that he ought to confess. All priests know that the enforcing of confession leads, terribly frequently, to sacrilege, and perhaps this fact alone justifies the act of the reformers in throwing the decision upon each man's own conscience. They refused to say that absolution was of equal importance with baptism and communion, but they did not refuse it the title of sacrament, for the Homilies call it one. They asserted truly that it had no outward Sign, or Matter, ordained by Christ, but so did the Council of Trent, which stated that its efficacy resides in its Form "I absolve thee". That Form the Church of England retained. Our reformers taught that "God hath given power and commandment to his Ministers, to declare and pronounce to his people, being penitent, the Absolution and Remission of their sins".[1] They included the gift of authority to absolve in the Form for the ordination of a priest. "Receive the Holy Ghost. Whose sins thou dost forgive, they are forgiven."[2] They found a place in the Prayer Book for the traditional Western Form of absolution. "Our Lord Jesus Christ, who hath left power to his Church to absolve all sinners, who truly repent and believe in him, of his great mercy forgive thee thine offences: And by his authority committed to me, I absolve thee from all thy sins."[3] There is no doubt about the doctrine. This very ancient form of absolution was retained by the Church of England in spite of the furious opposition of the Puritans.

But if that is so, what about the practice? If the reformers

[1] Morning and Evening Prayer.   [2] Ordination of a Priest.
[3] Visitation of the Sick.

allowed people to consult their own consciences as to whether they ought to make their confessions, did they give them any guidance in the matter? Most certainly they did. They envisaged two great crises in human life, one physical, one spiritual. The physical crisis was sickness. All illness is a warning from God that life in this world will come to an end, and that after death there is judgement. Our life here is a probation, and in sickness God is giving us a chance to ask ourselves what use we are making of our time of opportunity, what preparation we are making for eternity. Therefore the Prayer Book gives detailed instructions about what a priest is to do when he visits the sick. He is to help the patient to make his will and provide as far as he can for his dependants. He is to inquire whether he is in love and charity with all men and if he discovers any root of bitterness he is to do all he can to reconcile him with his neighbours. He is to question him about his faith. If he discovers that the patient has mortal sin upon his conscience—"any weighty matter"—he is to "move" him to make his confession. Then, if he judges that he is truly penitent, he is to absolve him with the Form already quoted.[1]

The second, and spiritual, crisis is communion. Our Lord told us that unless we ate his Flesh and drank his Blood we would be dead souls. St Paul warned us that to eat and drink unworthily is to become guilty of the body and blood of the Lord, to eat and drink damnation (judgement). Here then is our Lord telling us that we must communicate and St Paul telling us that it is a great sin to do so unworthily. If we know that we have sin on our consciences, what are we to do? The reformers answered "because it is requisite, that no man should come to the Holy Communion, but with a full trust in God's mercy, and with a quiet conscience; therefore if there be any of you, who by this means [self-examination] cannot quiet his own conscience . . . let him come to me, or to some other . . . Minister of God's Word, and open his grief . . . that he may receive the benefit of absolution."[2] The meaning of all this is quite clear. If after careful self-examination we find that we have not committed mortal sin then we may take to ourselves the general absolution pronounced in the services of the Church.

[1] Visitation of the Sick.
[2] Long Exhortation, Communion Service.

But if we find that we have "weighty matter" upon our consciences then we ought to confess it so that we may be given particular absolution. This is almost identical with what to-day the Church in France is teaching those who are responding to the Pope's exhortation to frequent communion.

Considering the bitterness which the subject has since aroused it is surprising to find that at the time of the Reformation there was practically no controversy about it. Men like Cranmer and Latimer made their confessions, and so did Bishop Andrewes, who was born just before the death of Edward VI, and Charles I. It was not until the Puritans began to separate from the Church of England that the stupid "no man must come between my soul and God" began to be heard. It was stupid because everybody with whom we have to do comes between our souls and God, sometimes for good, sometimes for evil. Confession continued to be a normal Church practice until the death of Queen Anne. With the coming of the Hanoverians, who were German Protestants, the dissenting dislike of confession began to find a home in the hearts of Churchmen. The great neglect of the Sacrament of Penance belongs to the eighteenth and nineteenth centuries, although the practice of such a man as Dr Johnson and widely read books of devotion, such as Nelson's *Whole Duty of Man*, prove that use of this sacrament never wholly ceased. But to whatever extent it may have been neglected, the Prayer Book has been a continual witness to orthodox doctrine about it. Where the universal Church had said something like "you must not take the risk of deciding whether you have committed mortal sin, but must go to confession before you receive communion", the Church of England has said "examine your conscience. If it is clear of grievous wilful sin, you may communicate. But if your conscience is uneasy then be very sure that our Lord has left a way in which you may be forgiven, so that you may communicate without scruple or fear."

Does this new attitude involve any heresy? It does not. The doctrine of the subject is unchanged. It must be acknowledged that, by removing the obligation, the Church of England has made possible the practice of to-day, when by far the greater number of its children never seek absolution at all. On the other hand,

compulsory confession has led at times to very grave and acknowledged evils. We maintain that to say to members of the Church
"you ought", instead of saying "you must" cannot possibly be an
act of schism. This is the only difference in this matter between
the Church of England and the Church of Rome. It concerns
practice only. The Prayer Book doctrine about the theory of the
Sacrament of Penance differs in no respect at all from that of the
whole Church.

CHAPTER 12

THE BLESSED SACRAMENT

WHAT is the essential truth about the Blessed Sacrament? There is no doubt that the Catholic Church teaches that in it there is a real presence of our Lord. If there is a real presence, then it is the overwhelmingly important fact. The bread and the wine, which were placed upon the altar, fade into complete insignificance. For many centuries the Church does not seem to have had any difficulty about this. St Paul, writing the first account of the institution of the Eucharist which has survived, tells us that it is a "common partaking [communion] of the body . . . the blood of Christ".[1] When the gospels came to be written they explained how at the Last Supper our Lord took the bread and blessed it and said "This is my body" and likewise the wine, saying "This is my blood". Towards the end of the first century St John, in the sixth chapter of his gospel, develops the idea inherent in St Paul's teaching, and tells us that our Lord said, "This is the bread which came down from heaven. . . . He that eateth my flesh and drinketh my blood dwelleth in me, and I in him."[2]

Close on the heels of these scriptural statements come the writers of the first century. St Ignatius (about 110) says that the Blessed Sacrament is "the flesh of our Saviour Jesus Christ, which suffered for our sins". St Justin Martyr (about 150) explains that "the food which is made Eucharist . . . is the flesh and blood of that Jesus who was made flesh". The witness comes from both East and West. St Gregory of Nyssa, about 350, wrote "the bread sanctified by the Word of God we believe to be transmuted (or transformed) into the Body of God and the Word", and St Ambrose of Milan, about the same date, "nature itself is changed by the benediction . . . before it is consecrated it is bread. When the words of Christ shall have been added, it is the Body of

[1] 1 Cor. 10.16.   [2] John 6.50,56.

Christ."[1] It is not necessary to believe that the whole of eucharistic theology was clear in the minds of men who could write like this, any more than it is necessary to believe that when St Thomas in the Upper Room cried out "My Lord and my God" he was conscious of all that Nicea meant when it declared that our Lord was "of one substance with the Father". But the final definition of our Lord's godhead was, so to speak, inherent in St Thomas' declaration, and the finished teaching of the Church about the Blessed Sacrament is contained, as an acorn contains an oak and nothing else, in our Lord's own words and in the writings of his earliest disciples.

Sooner or later it was as inevitable that men should ask questions about how the change took place, as it was that they should ask how a Person, who had lived so thoroughly a human life that he had died on a cross, could be God as well as man. Just as the Church was forced to the great Christological definitions in order to preserve the reality of the Incarnation, so was it compelled at last to define the manner of our Lord's presence in the Blessed Sacrament. It took many centuries of controversy to reach a satisfactory explanation. The definition, which was finally promulgated at the Council of Trent in 1564, is called Transubstantiation. This may be said to have won universal consent, for although the East does not like the term it teaches the doctrine, and it has even accepted the term on several occasions.

The difficulty is this. Our Lord said that the bread and wine were his Body and Blood and yet, after consecration, no human sense can perceive anything except bread and wine. But in the same way that the philosophical Greek doctrine of the Logos, or Word of God, helped the Church to understand how our Lord, although he was perfectly human, was also true God, so did the scholastic philosophy of matter help it to explain the Blessed Sacrament. The Schoolmen taught that "matter" consists of two things—substance and accidents. The accidents are all those qualities which can be discerned by any human sense. These "adhere" to a substance, which can never be isolated or examined. The substance is the fundamental, underlying *some-*

[1] All these passages are quoted by Pusey in the *Doctrine of the Real Presence.*

thing, which constitutes the thing and which makes it what it is. Thus a piece of wood has a substance, which may be called "woodenness", which can never be discovered, except through the accidents. These are such things as colour, taste, smell, hardness, corruptibility, shape, and "workability". When the bread and wine are placed upon the altar they have both the substance and the accidents of ordinary bread and wine. When, in obedience to our Lord's command they are consecrated, he himself takes the place of the substance, but all the accidents of bread and wine remain. The reality becomes the Body and Blood of our Lord, but these cannot be perceived by any human analysis, for all that man can ever perceive in any thing are accidents. As St Thomas Aquinas put it—"taste and touch and vision to discern Thee fail". It is only "faith, which comes by hearing" that can pierce the veil. This, and this alone, can know him present in the "breaking of the bread".[1] There is nothing materialistic about the doctrine. It is the clearest and most satisfactory explanation which has ever been found of the manner in which our Lord keeps his promise to be with us in the Blessed Sacrament. It is the substance of the teaching of the East, as well as the West, and it could well have been accepted by our reformers, except for one thing—it had been "vulgarized". During the later Middle Ages it was interpreted by ignorant people to mean that our Lord's presence was a carnal one. The body with which he ascended into Heaven was thought about in the terms of our earthly bodies. This misconception gave rise to horrible stories of hosts which cried as they were broken and of corporals spotted with blood. It was not transubstantiation, as officially defined, that our reformers had in mind when they rejected the term, "transubstantiation". It was the materialistic perversion of the doctrine in popular theology and custom which they attacked. It was this which "cannot be proved by Holy Writ; but is repugnant to the plain words of Scripture, overthroweth the nature of a Sacrament, and hath given occasion to many superstitions".[2] The carnal presence of popular belief did all these things, but the Tridentine definition did not. It ran:

in the august sacrament of the Holy Eucharist, after the consecration of the bread and wine, our Lord Jesus Christ, true God and man, is truly,

[1] Luke 24.35.   [2] Article XXVIII.

really and substantially contained under the form of those sensible things. . . . Because Christ our Redeemer declared that which he offered under the form of bread to be verily his own Body, therefore it has ever been a firm belief in the Church of God, and this Holy Synod doth now declare it anew, that by the consecration of the bread and wine, a conversion takes place of the whole substance of the bread into the substance of the Body of Christ our Lord, and of the whole substance of the wine into the substance of his Blood . . . the form only of the bread and wine remaining.[1]

This "form" which remains is the sum total of all the attributes which were ever there. It is not an illusion, for it still has all the "reality" which God ever gave it. So much is this the case that the Missal after consecration actually refers to the Host as *panis*, bread. "What we see, feel and taste in the Blessed Sacrament is real, for the accidents are real entities, and the accidents are all that the senses ever do perceive. It is, moreover, because the accidents remain that the Eucharist is a sacrament. They constitute the outward part—they are the sensible sign of that refreshment of the soul, which follows from a worthy reception of the sacrament."[2] "So far as the Articles condemn transubstantiation on the ground that it has been abused, then", as Bishop Gibson points out, "Christianity itself must go, for there is scarcely a doctrine which has not been perverted or abused."[3]

The doctrine is easier to accept to-day than it has been in the past. About one hundred years ago scientists taught that matter was made up of separate and distinct atoms, whose nature was quite different. For people who believed that to be true transubstantiation involved the miracle of transmuting atoms into something contrary to their very nature—a thing which seemed as fabulous as the philosopher's stone. But now we know that the substance of all matter is electricity. It is the same everywhere, and the different atoms are merely electricity arranged differently. In consequence transmutation, so far from being incredible, is continuously taking place. For those who believe in a God who creates, and who can see, as the latest scientific teaching asserts, that creation proceeds continuously through the unending bringing into being of atoms in their simplest form, which are changed

[1] Trent, Sess. XIII.   [2] *Catholic Dictionary*.
[3] Gibson, *Article XXVIII*.

into more and more complicated forms, the doctrine of transubstantiation is not very difficult to hold. There would seem to be no question that God could, if he wished, do upon our altars the same kind of thing which he is continually doing in the universe. The change in the substance of bread and wine can take place as readily, and as certainly "as hydrogen is being steadily converted into helium".[1] One substance is being continually converted into another. The substance of bread and wine therefore, from a purely scientific point of view, *can* be converted into the Body and Blood of Christ. It depends on whether God wishes to convert it. Our Lord said he did. "This is my body . . . my blood",[2] and he was "The Truth, who spake it".

What, then, did our reformers make of this doctrine of the Catholic Church? Mountains of books have been written to prove that they rejected it, or changed it in some way, but the surprising fact is that they made no change whatsoever. They repudiated a doctrine of transubstantiation which the Church had never taught officially. They rejected a term which, defined as they defined it, the Church also rejected. Their positive teaching was that of the whole Church.

On the Continent, at the time of the Reformation, four great heresies developed about the Blessed Sacrament. Luther broke away from the scholastic philosophy of matter, but he clung firmly to the literal meaning of our Lord's words. This gave him the doctrine of consubstantiation; the bread and wine remained in their natural substances but to them, after consecration, is added the Body and Blood of Christ. Calvin taught that in the Blessed Sacrament there is no real presence of our Lord, but that he gives himself to the faithful when they receive the bread and wine; "Christ breathes life into our souls, nay, diffuses his own life into us, though the real flesh of Christ does not enter us." He believed that the purpose of communion was to bring vividly to men's minds the memory of Calvary. Zwingli accepted the sacrament as a memorial, but he maintained that in no sense at all did the elements become, or convey, our Lord: his chief aim in instituting the sacrament was that it might be a means of uniting believers in love to one another through adherence to their common

[1] Hoyle, *Nature of the Universe.*   [2] Mark 14.22,24.

Saviour. Consubstantiation had very little appeal in England, but the other theories all made some impression upon our formularies. And rightly so, for all, on the positive side, were true. It was only their negations which were wrong. Therefore in Article XXVIII the Church of England progresses up from the low water mark of Zwingli to the Catholic Faith. The Blessed Sacrament is truly said to be "a sign of the love that Christians ought to have among themselves one to another" (Zwingli). But it is more than that. It is "a sacrament [that is to say, an outward and visible sign, given unto us by Christ himself] of our Redemption by Christ's death" (Calvin). But it is still more. It is a "partaking of the body of Christ and likewise the cup of blessing is a partaking of the blood of Christ". There is a Real Presence of our Lord in it. It is no mere symbol or sign, no mere remembrance of something in the past. It is no mere channel through which our Lord enters our souls. Communicants actually receive him. It is "the body and blood of Christ which are verily and indeed taken and received by the faithful"[1] When the Anglican priest communicates anyone, he is not taught to say anything about a sign, or a means of grace. He says "The Body . . . The Blood of our Lord Jesus Christ".[2]

This language is not incompatible with the fourth of the great Reformation heresies—Receptionism. This grew out of Calvinism and has proved to be the most dangerous of all the minimizing theories. In some ways it is like the Semi-Arianism of the fourth century, which recommended itself to many because it allowed eloquent things to be said about our Lord, while skirting around the problem of his true divinity. It avoided affirming that he was "of one substance with the Father". People who could say that he was "like God", or quote St Paul and say that he was "the express image of God", or even that he was of "like substance as the Father" felt, and said, that there was no further need to probe into the mystery of his being. But they were wrong for, as St Athanasius pointed out, only a Christ, who is of one substance with God, really and truly "God from God", can be a Saviour. If our Lord were not *that* the Incarnation would be meaningless. At best this would be a stepping-stone to polytheism. For the value of the Incarnation is bound up with the fact that God himself

---

[1] Church Catechism.   [2] Communion Service.

came to lost mankind. Unless our Lord is Very God of Very God, made true man, then God sent "someone else". In which case our Lord does not reveal God, he reveals someone else. He only reveals God, the love of God, the power of God, the forgiveness of God, when what we see in his face is the glory of God himself, and no other.

This point has been laboured because it has a very real bearing on the problem of the Blessed Sacrament. Receptionism skates around the problem of "what it is" to concentrate on "what it does". It insists that those who receive the outward signs really and truly receive our Lord himself. It is "the Body and Blood of Christ which are verily and indeed taken and received by the faithful in the Lord's Supper". What do we need more? Why peer into the mystery of the nature of a presence, which can be experienced through communion. This sounds as sensible, and as charitable, as Semi-Arianism sounded, but just as that heresy, if it had triumphed, because of the weakness of its intellectual foundation, would have degraded our Lord from the category of One who is to be worshipped, either to that of a good example, or to that of a secondary God, so does Receptionism eventually mean that our Lord is not to be adored in his sacrament. His real presence is to be sought in the hearts of faithful communicants, and not where he said it was to be found. Receptionism puts the emphasis in the wrong place—on us, on our faith, on our act, instead of on God. The Catholic doctrine places it on God. Our Lord is truly present in the Blessed Sacrament, not because we need him, or because we believe him to be there, but because he said he would be. He did not say, as Calvin suggested "this bread shall remind you of my Body" or even "this bread shall convey my life to you". Nor did he say "this bread shall be like my body" as the Semi-Arians might have said. Neither did he say "take and eat this bread and I will be in your heart" as the Receptionists suggest. He said "this is my Body".

It is worth while trying to make the point as clear as possible, for a great many people are unconscious Receptionists. It is because they are that they offer so much opposition to reservation and extra-liturgical services of devotion. The test question is not "what is received in the Blessed Sacrament?" It is "what is given?" What lies upon the altar after consecration and before communion begins? Both Catholics and Receptionists believe that after they make their communion our Lord is in their hearts. But where is he before they receive him? Is he present in the sense "where two or three are gathered together in my Name, there am I"; and is that all? Are the gifts lying on the altar no more than objects which our Lord is going to use as a means of uniting himself to the faithful, or are they the visible veils of his real, objective, presence with his Church? The test question is not "what is received?" but "what is given?"

The answer of the Prayer Book is absolutely clear. It is contained in Article XXVIII, which states that in the Blessed Sacrament "the Body of Christ is given, taken, and eaten". "Given." That means that our Lord's presence is objective, He is given, however we may receive him. He is there quite apart from our faith, or our reception. He is present in the Blessed Sacrament because he wills to be. The Church of England trusts his word, and delivers Holy Communion to its children, not with some remark about a sign or symbol, or that Christ will be with them if they partake rightly. They hear, as they receive, the ancient Catholic form, "The Body . . . The Blood of our Lord Jesus Christ". However they may receive him, it is our Lord himself who is given, and because he is given, he is there before we receive him. Because that is so, his presence under the visible veils is adorable. This word "given" means that in the terribly bitter controversy about the Blessed Sacrament our reformers took their stand with the Catholic Church. This is made doubly clear by the fact that they only had to translate the ancient Latin Form of communion quite literally to have one very susceptible to a receptionist interpretation. The old Form had read, "Corpus Domini . . . custodiat", which means "May the Body of the Lord . . . preserve". The reformers were good Latinists and must have deliberately dropped the "may" in order to emphasize Catholic doctrine.

But does not the Article go on to say that our Lord is given "only after a heavenly and spiritual manner"? Of course it does, for that is Catholic doctrine. The Church does not believe in a carnal and earthly presence, although many people in the Middle

Ages did. But our Lord could not be so present. His carnal body
was changed at the resurrection into a heavenly one, as, St Paul
tells us, all our bodies will be changed at the Last Day. The
spiritual body, which our Lord raised to the glory that was his
before the world began, is the same body as that which died on the
cross. But its properties are different. It is no longer corruptible.
It is freed from the limitations of time and space, otherwise it
could not have been present on the road to Emmaus and in the
Upper Room at approximately the same time, and it could not be
present at the same time upon the millions of the altars of the
world. He could not be with everyone of us "all the ways", as he
said he would be. Since the resurrection he has been present in
the sacrament of his love, and everywhere else, in his heavenly
body of eternity, which is not less real, but more real, because it is
spiritual. "The things which are seen are temporal; the things
which are not seen are eternal". Our Article states quite correctly
that "the Body of Christ is given, only after a heavenly and
spiritual manner", for that is the nature of his Body now.

The Article goes on to say that "the means whereby we
receive" the Body of Christ "is faith". That again is a thoroughly
Catholic statement. Our Lord himself is given, because it is his
will that he should be. But we receive what we are capable of
receiving. St Paul tells us that to eat and drink unworthily is not
to receive the Lord's Body. Our Lord is really present whenever
the Church obeys his command, and fulfils the conditions which
he laid down. He is present whatever members of a congregation
may believe, or think, or whatever may be the state of their souls.
But when they begin to receive him in communion the case
changes. It is possible to receive him so that he dwells in us and we
in him. It is possible to receive him, as St Paul warns us, so that
we eat and drink damnation (judgement). The point is made
clearly in the words of administration. "The Body of our Lord
Jesus Christ which was given for thee, preserve thy body and soul
to everlasting life." That is what God offers. That is what God
gives. But how do we take what is offered? To our souls' health,
or to our condemnation? That is up to us, and therefore our Church
continues "Take and eat this ["this"—that is to say "this which
you are given, the Body of Christ"] in remembrance that Christ

died for thee; feed on him in thy heart by faith with thanksgiving."
In every sacrament there are two essentials. There is that which
God does and there is the disposition with which we receive.
The sacrament not only must be "valid", it is also necessary that
it should be received rightly. Faith receives. But the presence is
not due to faith, which as Bishop Gibson states "never creates
nor bestows". It is due to God, who gives.

Therefore our Article states that "the means whereby we receive
[the Body and Blood of Christ] is faith". Of course it is. The
Epistle to the Hebrews says that we cannot come to God unless we
"believe that he is". He is there, whether we have faith or not.
But if we do not believe he exists, then he is not present *for us*.
If we are not in a state of grace, of which right faith is an essential
factor, we cannot receive the virtue of the sacrament. This is
clearly stated in Article XXIX. "The Wicked, and such as be
void of a lively faith, although they do carnally and visibly press
with their teeth (as St Augustine saith) the Sacrament of the Body
and Blood of Christ, yet in no wise are they partakers of Christ;
but rather, to their condemnation, do eat and drink the sign or
Sacrament of so great a thing." That is what St Paul said: "he
that eateth and drinketh unworthily, eateth and drinketh judgement unto himself, if he discern not the body."[1] But the body must
be there to be discerned. It is given, but not necessarily received,
to salvation. The Fathers echo this teaching over and over again.
Thus St Hilary says "the bread which cometh down from heaven
is not received except by him who is a true member of Christ".[2]
St Jerome says "these who are lovers of pleasure more than lovers
of God neither eat his Body nor drink his Blood".[3] St Ambrose
says "he receives who is worthy".[4] St Thomas Aquinas prays
that he may receive the "virtue and substance [*rem*]" of the
Sacrament.[5] Although there has been a little controversy in the
Church about what in very fact the wicked and unfaithful do
receive, there is universal agreement that only those who "receive
by faith" partake of the virtue of the sacrament.

[1] 1 Cor. 11.29.   [2] *De Trinitate*, VIII.   [3] In Esai 66.17.
[4] See also Gore on the Teaching of the Fathers in *The Body of Christ*
p. 144.
[5] Preparation for Communion.

But does not the Prayer Book actually call the consecrated elements Bread and Wine? For example: "when he [the Minister] delivereth the Bread to anyone, he shall say, 'The Body of our Lord'". The Church of England never refers to the Blessed Sacrament as bread and wine without capitals and it never refers to them as Bread and Wine except in rubrical directions. As we have seen, all we can perceive with our senses are the elements, the attributes, the appearances of bread and wine. What more natural, therefore, that when giving directions about how they are to be used, the terms which describe their appearance should be employed. The Roman missal calls the Host "Bread" in a prayer, a much more serious matter. It offers to God "the holy Bread of eternal life". But why not? Did not our Lord call himself "the true Bread"? Surely, if he could so refer to his human body, we can use the same term when referring to his eucharistic Body. And certainly if Rome can do so in a prayer and be blameless, Canterbury can do so in a rubric, without being condemned as heretical!

But there remains one difficulty, which to some people seems to contradict flatly all this argument. It is known as the Black Rubric and is printed at the end of the rubrics of the Communion Service, usually in especially dark type. It must be confessed that it is a deplorable explanation of why we kneel to receive communion. It is badly phrased and does little to-day save illustrate the bitterness with which a long dead controversy was fought. Since it is only a rubric it cannot make null and void teaching incorporated in the actual service, in the Catechism, or in the Articles. Its history is this. The second of the two regents who exercised the royal authority during the minority of Edward VI was the Duke of Northumberland, an extreme Protestant, who would have liked to reduce the Church of England to the status of a Genevan sect. All his sympathy, therefore, was on the side of a very noisy minority of Englishmen, who regarded Holy Communion as little more than a fellowship meal and desired to express this by sitting around the Lord's table. But although he would have liked to please these extremists, by making sitting at least a permissible posture, he dared not do so. The vast majority of the nation, which, of course, in those days was conterminous with the

Church, regarded the custom with horror. So he went as far as he
dared to please the extremists. He held up for some months the
publication of the Second Prayer Book in order that the Black
Rubric might be inserted. He seems to have written it himself.
Certainly it was inserted on his sole authority. Neither Convocation
nor Parliament was allowed to express an opinion, and the archbishop protested strongly against it. Although Northumberland
was compelled by public opinion to enforce kneeling, he hoped
that he could placate his Protestant friends by explaining that the
posture had no meaning.

The Second Prayer Book was in use only for some ten months.
Then came the reaction under Mary. Almost the first business to
be undertaken after the accession of Elizabeth was the issuing of
the Third Prayer Book, and in this the Black Rubric found no
place. Convocation was unanimous in rejecting it and Parliament
concurred. Under the Commonwealth, when the Church was suppressed, and the Prayer Book made illegal, sitting became the
usual posture for those partaking of the Lord's Supper. At the
Restoration, when the worship of the Church again became legal,
the Puritans wished to continue the Protestant custom and asked
that, if this should be disallowed and kneeling enforced, the Black
Rubric should again be inserted in the Prayer Book. The bishops
replied, "this rubric is not in the Liturgy of Queen Elizabeth, nor
is there any great need of restoring it, the world being now in more
danger of profanation than of idolatry."[1] Nevertheless, as a gesture,
intended to conciliate people who hated kneeling, they consented
finally to the insertion of an amended version. But before considering this, it will be as well to look at the rubric in its worst form.
It stated that by kneeling "it is not meant that any adoration is
done, or ought to be done, either unto the sacramental bread or
wine there bodily received, nor to any real and essential presence
there being of Christ's *natural* flesh and blood". At first sight this
is a denial of the real presence. But, as soon as it is examined, it is
clear that although it is expressed with abominable clumsiness, it
does not deny the Catholic faith. All are agreed that no adoration
ought to be paid to the "sacramental bread and wine". The
accidents of the sacraments are not adorable. Also, there cannot

[1] Savoy Conference.

be any "real and essential presence" of Christ's *natural* flesh and blood, because our Lord's "natural" flesh and blood have been changed into heavenly ones. It is not a natural body, as some medievalists supposed, but a spiritual body which is really and essentially present. We may confess that Northumberland skirted as near the edge of heresy as he could have done. But he just contrived to escape falling in. Perhaps he intended to frame a heretical statement. We are not concerned with his intentions, but with his actual words. They contrive to be orthodox, but they are so badly put together that we may thank God that this lay dictator's essay in theology never received any ecclesiastical, or even parliamentary, approval. Northumberland's rubric was never legal. In 1662 "real and essential" were changed to "any corporal presence".

As this rubric now stands it is quite orthodox. Catholics do not adore the outward signs of the sacrament, neither do they adore the natural, earthly, or carnal body of Christ. He is present in the Blessed Sacrament in the heavenly, spiritual body of eternity, which is not less, but more, real because it is spiritual. Material things have a limited reality and are all destined to pass away. Spiritual things are eternal. But to deny that the spiritual presence of our Lord in the Blessed Sacrament is real would involve the assertion that Heaven, even God himself, is not real.

Our reformers very strongly reacted against all carnal and materialistic theories of our Lord's presence in the Blessed Sacrament. The Council of Trent did so also, and all orthodox teaching has done the same. But the Prayer Book retained the Catholic doctrine of our Lord's objective presence amongst us, under the veils of bread and wine. By "veils", which is the characteristic Anglican term, the Church of England means something which is indistinguishable from the "accidents" of official Roman teaching. If anything like reasonable consideration is given to the Protestant doctrines of the Reformation period, and to the fierceness and bitterness with which they were urged upon our reformers, their fidelity to the Catholic faith appears to be little short of miraculous.

7

The Holy Sacrifice

The Catechism replies to the question of why the Blessed Sacrament was instituted, "for the continual remembrance of the sacrifice of the death of Christ and of the benefits which we receive thereby". What is this "remembrance of the sacrifice of the death of Christ"?

Our Lord had said that he came "not to destroy the law but to fulfil". It had all testified of him. The old sacrifices, which had been at its heart, had never been more than shadows, prefiguring the only possible true atonement—that offered to the Father by incarnate God himself, who took upon himself the sins of the world, and offered himself for them on the Cross. The old Covenant, sealed with the blood of many victims, was not abolished, but found meaning and fulfilment in the new, which was established in the blood of the Lamb of God. "Jesus took bread, and blessed, and brake it, and gave it to them, and said Take eat: this is my body. And he took the cup, and when he had given thanks, he gave it to them: and they all drank of it. And he said unto them, This is my blood of the new covenant",[1] "this do in remembrance of me".[2]

Up to this point almost all Christians, save Zwinglians, are in complete agreement. The Lord's Service is the memorial of the sacrifice of the death of Christ. It is the God-given way of holding up before men the memory of the one perfect and sufficient sacrifice which fulfilled all sacrifice.

But is it more than this? St Paul tells us that by it we "show forth the Lord's death till he come".[3] That might mean no more than we "proclaim to man". But it may equally well mean "remind the Father of the Lord's death". There is no doubt that from the first this latter interpretation was present in the mind of the Church. When our Lord instituted the Sacrament, St Paul and St Luke tell us that he used a word which we are accustomed to translate "do". "Do this in remembrance of me". But it can equally well mean "offer" and it is in that sense which the Church first understood it. By our Lord's death we were "reconciled to God" and he instituted the Blessed Sacrament that we might

[1] Mark 14.22.   [2] Luke 22.19.   [3] 1 Cor. 11.26.

plead that death in satisfaction for our sins. Therefore the very earliest liturgies call the Eucharist a sacrifice. It is expressly called one in the Didache (about 100). St Justin Martyr (about 150) says that Christians fulfil the prophesy of Malachi 1.10–12 "in that in every place they offer sacrifices to God, that is to say, the bread of the Eucharist and the cup of the Eucharist".[1] There can be no doubt at all that the primitive Church thought about the Eucharist as a sacrifice and believed that in it our Lord's Body and Blood were offered to the Father. It was a "showing forth" of the Lord's death, not only to men, but also to God.

But how can that be? The essence of sacrifice resides in an offering to God, which is destroyed so far as this world is concerned.[2] That is true even of those sacrifices which were eaten in part by the offerers. Living victims were killed and their typical parts burnt. How, then, is it possible to speak of our Lord as being offered in sacrifice upon the altars of the Church? It is because he becomes really present in the Sacrament of his love and that sacrament is consumed in communion. The Blessed Sacrament is destroyed *as itself*, although most certainly our Lord is not slain again.

The clue to the problem is found in the Epistle to the Hebrews. There we are told that in the Old Dispensation, after the victim of the atonement had been slain, the High Priest carried its blood, its life, through the Holy Place and passing through the great veil, presented it to God in the Holy of Holies. These were "figures of the true".[3] They typified the real sacrificial victim of the human race, the Lamb of God, who to take away our sins allowed himself to be slain on Calvary. He rose from the dead and ascended through the veil of material things, carrying the blood of his sacrifice, to appear in the presence of God. In the true Holy of Holies, now become our High Priest, he shows his precious Blood and "ever liveth to make intercession".[4] He died once for all, but his presentation of his sacrifice is a continual happening, which will continue until the need for it is over.

[1] *Dialogue with Trypho.*
[2] This is true even if, as some scholars think, the death of the victim was not central. The victim, by being taken up into God, was destroyed in this world. Cf. Appendix C.
[3] Heb. 11.24.   [4] Heb. 7.25.

Before he died he took the bread and wine and blessed them and said "This is my body . . . my blood. Offer them as a memorial of me". When we obey the command and offer the gifts of his appointing he takes them and identifies himself with them. He becomes really present under their veils. Because he ever liveth to intercede for us, by our obedience, we are caught up into his High Priestly intercession. Every Mass, from the point of view of earth, is separate and distinct. It is a renewal of the material offering which is commanded. But, from the point of view of Heaven, there is a continual happening into which men enter whenever they are obedient to the divine command. The Eucharist is not a sacrifice in the sense that the victim is slain anew. But it is one in that it enables us to share over and over again in a sacrifice, which is unceasingly pleaded in the heavenly places.

In the beginning the sacrifice was thought about as an act of the whole body of Christ on earth, in communion with angels and archangels and the Church expectant and triumphant. In it every member had a "liturgy", a service to perform. Bishops and priests, the divinely appointed representatives of the Body, were the actual consecrators, but they were not alone in offering the sacrifice; that was the act of the whole body of faithful; the Ministers acted with the body, not for it. The Mass was a collective action and some memory of this has survived in High Mass, although to-day even in that most of the laity play a very passive part. Three things combined to deprive them of the exercise of their priesthood. 1. The gradual disuse of Latin as the language of common speech. When the service came to be conducted in a dead language the laity were able to participate actively less and less. 2. The virtual abandonment of communion, except at Easter. 3. The introduction of Low Masses said by the priest, often with only one assistant. These changes shifted the ancient balance of the service and gave to the term "sacrifice" a popular meaning unknown in the early ages of the Church. They paved the way for great evils. Our Lord came down from heaven to be present under the veils of bread and wine to be "offered" by the priest. The thought became intolerable when his presence was imagined as a carnal, or earthly one. Such a presence was taught by at least one Pope. Nicholas II in 1059 forced Berengar of Tours to assent to a statement that "the bread and wine placed on the altar are after consecration not only a sacrament, but also the true Body and Blood of our Lord and these are sensibly handled and broken by the hands of priests and crushed by the teeth of the faithful, not only sacramentally, but in reality".[1] It is not surprising that such an opinion should have given rise amongst the ignorant to stories of hosts which bled when broken. Just as heretical was a doctrine that the Mass supplemented the sacrifice which our Lord offered on Calvary. There is a good deal of evidence for the teaching that while the cross atoned for original sin, the atonement for actual sin, both mortal and venial, was effected by the sacrifice of the Mass.

Our reformers were faced by popular errors of faith and by customs very different to those of the universal Church. They reacted violently. Even so they did not overstate their case. They emphasized the truth that there is but one sacrifice which atones for sin and that is the one offered on Calvary. They stated that "there is none other satisfaction for sin but that alone".[2] This is good Catholic doctrine. Article XXXI continues "the sacrifices of Masses, in the which it was *commonly* said [the Latin is *vulgo dicebatur*, which means something like "said by the ignorant"] that the Priest did offer Christ for the quick and the dead, to have remission of pain or guilt, were blasphemous fables, and dangerous deceits": this is also a Catholic statement. The conception of the priest making our Lord present and offering, or even sacrificing by slaying, him over and over again is wholly false. It is this "sacrifice of Masses"—note the plural—which is stigmatized as a blasphemous fable. Our reformers did not assert that there is no sense in which the Mass can be called a sacrifice. They did not contradict the definition of the Council of Trent which was promulgated nearly ten years later. This stated simply that the Mass is "truly propitiatory both for the living and the dead". Of course it is, for all prayer in the Name and through the merits of our Saviour is truly propitiatory, and no prayer is so complete an entering into and appropriating the benefits of his passion as is the institution whereby we "dwell in him and he in us". Nowhere at all does the Church of England deny that the Eucharist is a sacrifice in the

[1] Quoted Gibson, *XXXIX Articles*.   [2] Article XXXI.

true sense. The Church of England prays that God will accept "this our sacrifice of praise and thanksgiving".[1] That does not mean the prayers and praises which have been uttered. It means "this our Eucharist". It is a technical term taken from the ancient liturgies.

What our reformers did was to go back behind the medieval corruptions of sacrificial doctrine to the faith and practice of the primitive Church. The Anglican Eucharist is a memorial made to God the Father of the atoning blood shed for us on Calvary. It is a pleading of the merits of that blood together with him who shed it for us. Even a casual glance at the Prayer of Consecration will show how the Prayer Book insists upon this. "Almighty God . . . who . . . didst give thine only Son . . . to suffer death upon the Cross for our redemption; who made there (by his one oblation of himself once offered) a full, perfect, and sufficient sacrifice, oblation, and satisfaction, for the sins of the whole world; and did . . . command us to continue, a perpetual memory of that his precious death . . . Hear us, O merciful Father, we most humbly beseech thee". In that prayer, who are we reminding of Calvary and its effects? Ourselves? No, we are speaking to the Father. We are reminding him of what his Son did for us. In St Paul's words we are "showing forth the Lord's death" *to him*.

Although our reformers made it absolutely impossible for any Anglican to think that in the Mass a victim is slain, they did teach that it is a sacrifice in which a victim is offered, by God's express command. As we have seen, the real point about the Blessed Sacrament is that it is our Lord himself. It is he himself, under the eucharistic veils, who is present with us, and he is present so that, with him, we may plead his merits. In no way is there any repetition of his sacrifice on Calvary. We add nothing to that. We plead an accomplished sacrifice which is consummated by communion. By our reception of his precious Body and Blood, the Blessed Sacrament is destroyed as itself. By that destruction the sacrifice is completed, and this is true even if the essence of sacrifice be a "taking up into God", for by communion that is what is effected—"we dwell in him and he in us".

There is, or used to be, a Protestant saying to the effect that

[1] Prayer of Oblation.

the reformers turned a sacrifice into a communion. The suggestion is utter nonsense, for the Mass is a sacrifice only because it is a communion. If there were no communion there would be no sacrifice. But there always is a communion, for at least the priest always communicates, and therefore there is always a sacrifice.

What our reformers tried to do was not to take the sacrifice out of the communion but to bring the congregation into the sacrifice. This is the reason for the rubrics at the end of the Communion Service which try to make compulsory the presence of a congregation who communicate with the priest. But English folk are stubborn and these regulations failed. In fact they produced a result far different from their intention. People who did not wish to communicate simply stayed away from Mass.

But although the method chosen produced an unhappy result, no fault can be found with the motive. Our reformers wanted to get away from the practice and belief that the priest did something for the people, instead of with the people. They saw that the true belief is that it is the whole body of the faithful who offer the sacrifice, and they do so by communicating. This is a wholly Catholic idea, and Rome also is trying to recover it. Pope after Pope has stressed the duty of frequent communion, and to-day on the Continent it is possible to see large crowds communicating at High Mass, a thing which was almost unknown not many years ago. Our reformers were a little in advance of the Pope, but that did not make them heretics!

There is another point of great importance which our reformers stressed. What is the true substance of the matter which we offer to God? What do the "bread and wine which the Lord hath commanded to be received" mean? From the second century at least the Church taught that they represented the people who offered them. St Augustine, for example, declares that the bread and wine, which were then contributed by the faithful themselves, and brought to be placed on the altar at the offertory, represented the offerers. He says "there are you in the bread. There are you in the wine".[1] In the Middle Ages people had forgotten that they had anything to do at all. Their actual offering of the elements had long been given up and just as they had come to think of the

[1] Quoted Dix, Shape of the Liturgy.

priest as the sole sacrificer, so did they think of our Lord as the
only victim. Our reformers attempted to get back to the more
Catholic conception. The bread and wine represent ourselves.
The Christian body lays itself on the altar that it may become the
Body and Blood of Christ and be sacrificed. Our reformers taught
us to pray something essentially true, which the medieval Church
had forgotten. "And here we offer and present unto thee, O
Lord, ourselves, our souls and bodies, to be a reasonable, holy,
and lively sacrifice unto thee."[1] Our redeemed selves, all that we
are, our whole beings, symbolized by the bread and wine, are
placed upon the altar, and offered to God. They become an
acceptable offering when our Lord unites himself to us, first by
making the bread and wine his Body and Blood and then by giving
himself to us in communion.

As Bishop Christopher Wordsworth pointed out long ago the
Church of England has all the forms of sacrifice which the
scholastic theologians catalogued, except one. "It rejected what
the schoolmen called a *sacrifice supplitivum*, an additional sacrifice,
a repeated sacrifice, whereby some supposed defect in the sacrifice
of Calvary could be supplied."[2] But Rome itself has denied that
anything can be added to the completeness of Christ's offering of
himself on Calvary, or that in the Mass he is sacrificed again, or
that what he did for us can be either increased or repeated.[3] In
fact, if allowance is made for the fact that Rome uses the term
transubstantiation to mean one thing and our reformers used it to
mean another, and that they attacked popular superstitions, not
official doctrine, then the teaching of the Church of England is
seen to be the same as that of the Council of Trent.

The Holy Communion

Beyond all question, our reformers left the Church of England
with completely orthodox teaching and practice about Holy Communion. They found the faithful satisfied with annual communions
and they tried to encourage them to receive at least weekly. In
every possible way they stressed the importance of frequent

[1] Prayer of Oblation.   [2] Wordsworth, *Theophilus Anglicanus*.
[3] Trent Sess. XIII.

reception and in this not only returned to the most ancient custom of the Church, but also they anticipated papal policy by some centuries. They taught that in communion the Body and Blood of Christ are given, taken, and received. They gave excellent advice about how to prepare, especially in the exhortations of the communion service. They warned communicants very plainly about the danger of unworthy reception, and reminded them that our Lord had provided a remedy in absolution.

Our reformers' doctrine of the effects of communion was impeccable. Our Saviour "hath instituted and ordained holy mysteries, as pledges of his love, and for a continual remembrance of his death, to our great and endless comfort".[1] The benefits of a good communion, they taught, are twofold. First, by it we are united to our Lord who is the "propitiation for our sins". "Grant us, therefore, gracious Lord, so to eat the Flesh of thy dear Son Jesus Christ, and to drink his Blood, that our sinful bodies may be made clean by his Body, and our souls washed through his most precious Blood and that we may evermore dwell in him and he in us."[2] The reference to our Lord's words are unmistakable; "Whoso eateth my flesh and drinketh my blood dwelleth in me and I in him." Secondly, through communion we are united with all his other members in the body of the Church. St Paul told us that, by virtue of our communions, we, "being many, are one bread, one body: for we are all partakers of that one bread".[3] Thus our Prayer Book declares, "Almighty and everlasting God, we most heartily thank thee, for that thou dost vouchsafe to feed us, who have duly received these holy mysteries, with the most precious Body and Blood of thy Son, our Saviour, Jesus Christ, and dost assure us thereby . . . that we are very members incorporate in the mystical body of thy Son."[4] Union with Christ, who is our atonement, from whom, as the branches of a vine draw life from the vine, we draw forgiveness, life, health, and strength, and union with the Catholic Church, that comprehends everything which can possibly be effected by communion. It sums up all the faith of the Church about the efficacy of the Blessed Sacrament.

[1] Third long Exhortation. [2] Prayer of Humble Access.
[3] 1 Cor. 10.17. [4] Prayer of Thanksgiving.

But our reformers did make one change in what had been the accepted custom of the Western Church for over three hundred years. They restored the chalice to the laity. Communion in one kind only had been first condemned, then tolerated and at last enforced. There is no doubt that in the very beginning the laity communicated in both species. St Paul's words are sufficient proof. "Let a man examine himself and so let him eat . . . and drink."[1] Passage after passage from the Fathers could be quoted to show that the laity received the chalice as a matter of course, when they communicated in church. Indeed, the first reference to reception of the Lord's Body alone comes from Pope Leo I, about 440, who declared that the custom of certain Manicheans of refusing the chalice was "a sacrilegious deceit for which they were to be expelled from the fellowship of the saints".[2] Communion in one kind was condemned by the Council of Claremont under Pope Urban II in 1095. But, in spite of condemnation, the custom spread throughout the West, until it was made the rule at the Lateran Council in 1215. Later at the Council of Constance in 1415, not without some obvious embarrassment, an attempt was made to justify it. "Though Christ instituted and gave this sacrament to his disciples under both kinds, yet the Church has the power of ordering that to the laity it be given in one kind only."[3] The Council then proceeded to exercise this power to make a change in a divine command by again forbidding the chalice to be administered to the laity. By this act the Westerns made it still more difficult to heal the schism which divided them from the East, and they departed from the tradition of the universal Church.

It is worth noting that, although the Council of Trent confirmed this decision, yet Rome has never attempted to force communion in one kind on the oriental schisms which have submitted to the Papacy. Like the Orthodox East, they still administer communion in both kinds. Therefore when our reformers restored the cup to the laity all they broke away from was a novel and bad custom of the West. It is not necessary to deny the truth of the doctrine on which communion in one kind is based, that is that our Lord who is one person, cannot be partly present in the Bread and partly

[1] 1. Cor. 11.28.   [2] Homily XLI.   [3] Conc. Const. Sess. XIII.

present in the Wine, and therefore he must be received wholly under both species. We need condemn neither Rome, nor this doctrine, which is called concomitance. But for the Church of England to return to the ancient custom of the universal Church can hardly be stigmatized as an act of schism which separated it from that Church!

The Reformed Service

It is very certain that the compilers of the Prayer Book intended to frame a service which would express, not a new doctrine, but the ancient Catholic faith about the Blessed Sacrament. Their service was to be a service of "The Church". They provided the three traditional essentials for validity, Minister, Matter, and Form. No one was to be permitted to celebrate save one who had been episcopally ordained. It has always been a sore point with the Protestant sects that while the Church of England accepts as valid Roman orders and allows priests who have received them to celebrate at its altars, it has always insisted that nonconformist ministers should be episcopally ordained before they are suffered to do so. Throughout the service of Holy Communion the term Priest is used whenever any reference is made to the actual celebrant. Terms such as "the Curate", and "the Minister", always refer to some assistant, other than the celebrant. Thus the Curate shall give out the notices, but it is the Priest who makes the offertory. The general confession is to be made by "one of the Ministers", but it is the Priest who is to turn to the people and pronounce absolution. This principle is enforced everywhere. The service envisages various "assistants", but the actual celebrant must be a Priest. The Matter of the sacrament is "bread and wine which the Lord hath commanded to be received".[1] The Prayer Book suggests that in accordance with the custom of the West, wafer bread will normally be used but, mindful of the use of the Eastern churches, it declares that ordinary wheaten bread suffices, provided it is the best that can be obtained.[2] The wine, of course, is ordinary fermented wine. The Protestant custom of using grape juice had not arisen. If it had, there is no doubt that our reformers would

[1] The Catechism.   [2] Rubric before Communion Service.

have reacted violently against it. They were certainly not Manicheans. The Form which they continued is that which the Western Church has used from the earliest times, our Lord's words of institution. There is a very considerable controversy in the Church about whether these words, or a prayer that the Holy Ghost should make the bread and wine the Body and Blood of Christ, is the earliest and true Form, and East and West are divided about it. But the East, which has both Forms, does not seem to deny completely the validity of the Western use, which fixes its eyes on the words of institution as the moment of consecration. Our reformers continued the Western use. They provided a prayer that the bread and wine might convey the Body and Blood of the Saviour and they accepted so completely the words of institution as effecting consecration that they ordered their bare repetition, if the Body, or the Blood, became exhausted before the end of the general communion. Some Anglicans regret this whole-hearted acceptance of Western teaching about the Form of consecration, but assuredly Rome has no right to blame us.

Our reformers did three main things with the service which they had inherited. 1. They simplified it by pruning away all the "proper" except the collect, epistle, and gospel. 2. They rewrote most of the "ordinary" and rearranged it. 3. They retained all the old "points" of the service.

1. The new matter is unexceptionable. Some of the new collects are far better than the ones which they replaced. Compare, for example, the new collect for Advent Sunday with the old. But most of the variable parts of the service which were retained were straightforward translations of the old. We can acknowledge that the reformers' love for simplicity amounted almost to mania, and that the result of their pruning away of the "proper" was the destruction of all the light and shade of our services. Except for collect, epistle, and gospel the service of Ash Wednesday, for example, is almost the same as that for Easter Day. But to say that we cannot share the sixteenth-century craze for drabness is not to accuse our rite of lack of validity. No part of the Church turns to the variable proper for the proof of validity.

2. However keenly some Anglicans may regret the breaking up of the old order of the service, which had been used in England

from the time of St Augustine, this in itself, could not have constituted a breach of Catholic unity. The new matter is completely orthodox. It is not heretical to mingle an Old Testament lesson (the commandments) with the Kyries, or to add a prayer to each ancient petition for mercy. It is not heretical to replace the ancient "secret prayers" with an intercession for the Church. The new confession and absolution and the Prayer of Humble Access and the Comfortable Words, are not heretical. The new prayers of Consecration, Oblation, and Thanksgiving contain nothing for which Catholics need apologize. We may dislike intensely the removal of the Gloria in Excelsis from its ancient place at the beginning of the service, but it cannot be regarded as heretical to sing it (following the example of our Lord and the apostles in the upper room) as a hymn before going out into the world. Not one sentence in the new matter presents a Catholic with an embarrassing expression.

3. Our reformers retained all the old landmarks of the Catholic liturgy. The new service has the two ancient divisions. There are clearly distinguishable Masses of "the Catechumens" and of "the Faithful". The former is almost identical with that of the Middle Ages. The latter begins, in accordance with tradition, with the offertory. From the third century the placing of the bread and wine on the altar was often accompanied by prayer. In the new rite this was dropped, but as the oblations were placed on the altar at the accustomed time, the congregation would not have noticed much change, for the prayers had been said secretly. A Roman Catholic authority says the custom of the first three centuries shows that "they used to perform the whole of that action in silence, considering that the prayers contained in the canon were sufficient, as indeed they are".[1] The Sursum Corda and Sanctus lift the action in the ancient way into Heaven. The words of institution effect the consecration. There is a "fraction". The communion of priest and people consummate the sacrifice. This is followed by thanksgiving and a dismissal blessing in the medieval manner. All the points of the Western rite are present, although the order is changed. We may regret this dislocation of that old and venerable order, indeed we may resent it bitterly, but it cannot

[1] Martène, *De Ant. Ecc. Rit.*

be maintained that a service which contains all the old landmarks is anything but a rite of the Church. It may be that our reformers carried to extremes, which it is very difficult to justify, their doctrine that a national Church has the right to do the things which the Catholic Church does, according to its own "use". But that does not mean that, in itself, the contention is wrong—how could it be, in view of the fact that in the East all the national Churches have their own distinctive liturgies (as have also the Uniat Churches)? The only questions which it is reasonable to ask about the new use of the Church of England are "is it celebrated by a valid ministry, with valid Matter and Form?"; "does it contain a sufficiency of the traditional elements to make it clear that it is in truth a rite of the Catholic Church?"; "is it framed in such a way that it effects the consecration of the bread and wine so that they become the Lord's Body and Blood?"; "does it plead before the Father the 'sacrifice of the death of Christ'?"[1]; "does it make clear that the communicants are united to our Lord, and to his whole Body, and that they become partakers of the merits of his atoning sacrifice?" There is not the slightest possible doubt that those questions can only be answered in the affirmative.

[1] The Catechism.

CHAPTER 13

HOLY MATRIMONY

MARRIAGE is an institution of natural law conterminous with humanity. Anthropologists tell us that custom about it has greatly varied, but we know that, in the plan of God, marriage has always been the lifelong union of one man with one woman to the exclusion of all others. Our Lord said that at the beginning God made male and female and that because of his will "they twain . . . are no more twain but one flesh". This marriage, this union of two people so as to make "one flesh", is not a temporary, but a lifelong attachment. "What therefore God hath joined together, let not man put asunder."[1] When our Lord enunciated this doctrine his apostles were horrified. "If a man can't get rid of his wife for any cause at all", they argued, "then he is a fool to marry."[2] Our Lord answered them by reiterating God's law clearly and unequivocally. He said that to put away a wife or husband and to take another partner was not to marry again but to commit adultery. Sometimes this law enforcing the indissolubility of the marriage bond is spoken of as the law of the Church. It is much more than that. Our Lord's words prove that it is the law of God.

The Jews and the heathen both allowed divorce in certain circumstances. In consequence when they married they did not enter into a lifelong contract. The first problem which the Church had to face grew out of that fact. When a man or woman becomes a Christian and the other spouse does not, what is to happen? St Paul answered that if both, in spite of the difference of religion, desired to continue as man and wife they were to do so. But if the unbelieving partner of the marriage wished to claim the privilege of the pre-Christian custom, then the marriage should be annulled, and in that case the Christian should be free to contract a real marriage. The heathen and Jewish marriage ceremony, bereft as it was of the lifelong intention, was not a true

[1] Matt. 19.5,6.   [2] Matt. 19.10.

marriage. St Paul stated that he had not divine authority for this ruling. It was his private opinion. On the other hand he was quite clear that when two Christians married it was for life, and that divorce was sin. This, he said, was of God.[1]

The law remained unchanged until the conversion of Constantine. When the Church was invaded by hosts of people, who were not Christians at heart, it became irksome. Under pressure from the emperors, and semi-pagan magnates, it was relaxed more and more, until in the East divorce was allowed for a large number of causes. The situation was parallel to that amongst the Jews in the time of our Lord. The law of God was clear, but emperors and bishops, like Moses, for the "hardness of men's hearts",[2] allowed divorce. In course of time the Eastern theologians invented a theory of marriage to whitewash this corrupt following of Christ. They said that a marriage could "die". When that happened it was the same thing as if one of the partners to it died. Therefore the couple could be separated and marry again. The West never descended to such sophistry, but it also found a way of condoning what our Lord had said was sin. The legal western mind placed all the emphasis on the contractual aspect of the ceremony. Any contract, to be valid, must comply with certain legal requirements. For example, a will must be properly witnessed, and a receipt for payment above a certain sum must be stamped. The ecclesiastical lawyers insisted that for marriage to be legal it must fulfil certain conditions—the contracting partner must be free to marry; minors are not free without consent of parents or guardians; nor are people who stand to one another in certain degrees of relationship. The contract, also, must be duly made in the authorized form, and properly witnessed. It must be possible to prove that the parties knew what they were doing, and that they really intended to marry. All these points gave opportunity for breaking marriages, as when Henry VIII pleaded that he had never been properly married to Catherine of Aragon, because she was his brother's widow and therefore was related to him in a prohibited degree. The result of this legalism was very much the same as the pretence of the Easterns. But it had one advantage. It preserved the letter of the law, which our Lord had pronounced.

[1] Cf. 1 Cor. 7.   [2] Matt. 19.8.

Both East and West taught that marriage was a sacrament in that through it God bestowed the grace to make it a success, but they developed different doctrines about who was the Minister of the sacrament. The East taught that he was the priest who imparted the nuptial blessing. The West adopted the custom of Roman civil law. This is perfectly exemplified still in Scottish law, which accepts as valid any declaration of marriage made anywhere in Scotland, at least by people of Scottish blood, without previous notice of any kind, so long as it is made before witnesses, who need have no official position at all. The dangers of abuse to which this law opens the way are obvious. Therefore the West came to demand some official witness and almost always this would be a priest or bishop, although it retained the idea that the parties themselves are the Ministers. The Council of Trent went still further and decreed that no marriage was to be accounted valid unless celebrated by the parish priest, or by someone authorized by him. This is still the Roman Catholic law and although it brings the custom of the West into line with that of the East, nevertheless it is a departure from the ancient position of the Roman Church, and to some extent obscures the fact that marriage is an institution of natural, not just of ecclesiastical, law.

There has never been any universally agreed Matter of the sacrament, for Christians carried on with what had been the customs of their countries. Whatever has been customary in any place has always been accepted as valid. The Form in the West used to be the promise of the parties to be man and wife "till death us do part". To-day the Roman Church presumably finds it in the pronouncement of the officiating minister that the couple are man and wife.

What changes did our reformers make? None whatsoever, except that they remained truer to the old Roman tradition of the Minister than the Council of Trent did. They continued to insist on publicity as a safeguard for the bride, by ordering the publication of banns on three successive holidays (now Sundays), when the maximum number of people would hear them. They drew up a form of service, in which all the important parts are translations of the old Latin services, omitting nothing of substance, but adding valuable explanatory matter. They retained a "joining of hands

8

and giving and receiving of a ring" as the customary Matter of the sacrament. For the Form they continued the ancient promise made by both parties to take one another as husband and wife "till death us do part". They continued the ancient pronouncement of the priest that since the parties have consented together in holy wedlock, and signified the same by the accepted outward forms, they are husband and wife. The lifelong character of their contract is then emphasized by the solemn declaration that those whom God has joined together are not to be separated by man. At every point the Catholic doctrine of marriage is taught and it is solemnized with customary prayers and actions. It is noteworthy that there are signs that people who are campaigning for a laxer law of marriage are beginning to realize that "remarriage" after divorce is wholly incompatible with the Prayer Book service.

There is, in fact, only one point to which any kind of objection can be raised. That is the refusal of Article XXV to call Holy Matrimony a sacrament. This is purely a matter of definition. There is no Form or Matter connected with marriage which, by any stretch of imagination, can be said to have been "ordained by Christ", and the only sense in which he can be said to have instituted the sacrament is that as the second Person of the Blessed Trinity it was part of his plan for mankind. In essence marriage is, as the Article asserts, a state of life which is in accordance with his will. On the other hand our reformers called it a sacrament in the Homilies and most certainly they did not deny, and never intended to deny, that through it God gave the grace necessary to enable men and women to "please him both in body and soul, and live together in holy love unto their lives end". It would be fantastic to maintain that with regard to Holy Matrimony the Church of England broke away from either the doctrine, or the practice, of the Church.

CHAPTER 14

THE CARE OF THE SICK AND DYING

OUR LORD and his apostles seem to have accepted the whole body of doctrine and practice of the Jews with regard to sickness. They believed that when it was not a punishment for sin, it was the result of the malice of the devil. Our Lord called Satan the Prince of this world[1] and he said that it was he who had "bound"[2] the paralytic woman. St Peter said that the devil "as a roaring lion, walketh about, seeking whom he may devour".[3] That the evil which he works is not only spiritual is shown by the fact that St Paul called his "thorn in the flesh" "a messenger of Satan".[4] Our Lord proved by his acts that it was the will of God that men should strive to combat evil in all its forms, including bodily disease, and he gave his apostles the definite command to "heal the sick".[5]

How were they to carry out that commission? We cannot say with certainty. So far as we know there was no dominical instruction as to method. One thing however is certain. All healing of the sick must be a sacramental act, for God alone can heal. No medical science, no skill of doctor or surgeon, no power of drugs, no care of nurses can heal, apart from the blessing of God. Just as he alone gives life, so he alone can restore or preserve health. But although he is the actual source of all healing, nevertheless, as a rule, he works through agents and instruments. That is to say there is usually a "sacrament" of healing. Sometimes that is "medical science" and sometimes God achieves his purpose more directly in answer to prayer, or through an "ecclesiastical" sacrament. It must have been as ministers of a sacrament of the Church that our Lord commanded the apostles to heal, for they were neither doctors nor surgeons.

How did they administer a sacrament of healing? Sometimes

---

[1] John 14.30. [2] Luke 13.16. [3] 1 Pet. 5.8.
[4] 2 Cor. 12.7. [5] Matt. 10.8.

by pronouncing a word of power—"in the Name of Jesus Christ of Nazareth rise up and walk".[1] Sometimes, probably, by laying-on-of-hands after the example of our Lord. This was a natural adaptation of the Old Testament thought of the hand of God being stretched out to heal. Thus Jairus said to our Lord "my . . . daughter lieth at the point of death: I pray thee come and lay thy hands on her that she may be healed; and she shall live".[2] It was reasonable to suppose that our Lord's healing power would be poured out through the hands of the ambassadors whom he had commissioned to carry on his healing work. Sometimes, as St James shows us,[3] it was carried on through an anointing with oil. This also was an inheritance from the custom of the Jews. It is more than likely that usually all three methods would be employed. At some very early date, if not from the very first, to these was added communion of the sick. In the very first account of the Eucharist which has been preserved for us (Justin Martyr about 150) we are told that after the faithful have been communicated the deacons carry portions of the Blessed Sacrament to the sick. We know that by the end of the second century it was the custom for the clergy to visit the sick frequently, daily if that was possible, in order to communicate them with the reserved sacrament, and to anoint them with oil so that the healing power of God might be manifested.

The purpose of all this activity was restoration to health. St James said "the prayer of faith shall save the sick and he shall be raised up".[4] That was the main objective; but there was a subsidiary one also. Soul and body are constantly reacting on one another. Therefore, just as our Lord forgave the sins of the paralytic, before restoring to him the use of his legs, so does St James link together healing of body with healing of soul. "The Lord shall raise him up; and if he have committed sins, they shall be forgiven him."[5] This mixture of bodily and spiritual healing was always present in the mind of the Church, for it is the whole person that God was incarnate to save, and it is profitless to heal the body unless the soul is healed also.

This sacramental way of dealing with the sick by prayer and

[1] Acts 3.6.   [2] Mark 5.23.   [3] Jas. 5.14,15.
[4] Ibid.   [5] Ibid.

unction for healing of body and soul has always been the custom in the East. The rite is repeated over and over again until the patient recovers, or dies. The Roman Pontifical still bears witness to the similarity which first existed in the teaching of both West and East. Oil is still blessed "for the expulsion of all pains, all infirmities, and every sickness of body". A change in the meaning of anointing is usually traced back to Peter Lombard who, about 1150, wrote about the anointing of people *in extremis*, "on the point of death". It speedily became the custom to give unction only to such people, and the Council of Trent officially confined it to them by forbidding its use more than once in the same illness. Thus a service, which originally was intended to restore health, became a "sealing for death". The East protests strongly against this development as a departure from the apostolic tradition.

The changed outlook upon the purpose of unction led to another service, the Visitation of the Sick, becoming the normal way of ministering to ordinary sick folk. The Latin rite is very beautiful. Its psalms are full of trust and hope and its lessons tell the stories of some of our Lord's miracles of healing. It includes a laying-on of the priest's hand while quoting our Lord's words "they shall lay hands on the sick, and they shall recover".[1] All the prayers look forward to giving God thanks for recovery. This service preserves all the old doctrine of unction—but unction has been removed from it, to be reserved as a sacrament for the dying.

Hand in hand with this change in the purpose of unction went a change of doctrine. We have seen that in the thought of St James forgiveness of sins was a secondary effect of the sacrament and that this must be so. Now, this secondary function became primary. Although the prayers of the sacrament still reflect the earlier teaching, the actual Form with which it is administered speaks only of forgiveness. Each sense is anointed—head, eyes, nose, ears, mouth, hands, feet—using the form "by this holy anointing the Lord forgive thee all thy sins of thinking"—or seeing, smelling and so on. Thus unction came to be administered in order to secure the complete freeing of the soul from every stain. Many medieval teachers held that, when received with proper dispositions, it secured the soul immediate entrance into Heaven, so to

[1] Mark 16.18.

speak, by-passing purgatory. Both St Thomas Aquinas and Duns Scotus taught this doctrine and Pope Alexander III declared that extreme unction confers in the future life a degree of bodily glory not to be attained without it.

Unction, in fact, once it had lost its original motive, took to itself the properties which have always been rightly attributed to the Viaticum. From the beginning that had been the Christian's preparation for death. As early as the end of the first century, St Ignatius calls the communion, which he hopes to receive before martyrdom, "the medicine of immortality". The title grows naturally out of reflection upon our Lord's words "he that eateth my flesh and drinketh my blood hath eternal life; and I will raise him up at the last day".[1] The Council of Nicea decreed "concerning the dying, let the ancient and canonical rule still be kept: that none be deprived at the hour of death of the most necessary Viaticum". The longing of Christians to receive the Blessed Sacrament in this last hour was so great that it found its way into the ancient Eastern liturgy of St Basil. "Grant unto us at our last breath to receive worthily our share of Thy hallowed gifts as a Viaticum of eternal life, for an acceptable defence before the awful judgement seat." So important was it held to receive the Viaticum at the very last that it was allowed to be administered to a person who had already received communion on the same day. Although, even in the West, penance, when possible, and communion were administered in connection with extreme unction, this was not always so. In actual practice unction took the place of the Viaticum as the sacrament of the dying.

This "corrupt following of the apostles"[2] led to still more serious abuses. A belief grew up that after extreme unction a sick person *ought* to die. Naturally this led often to a deliberate postponement of the sacrament until hope of recovery had been completely abandoned and often until consciousness had gone. If the anointed person did by any chance recover he was supposed to live as if he was dead to the world, to fast perpetually, to walk barefoot, to avoid all amusements, to live in separation from wife or husband. In some places wills made by such people were invalid. Another crying abuse was that because this sacrament

[1] John 6.54. [2] Article XXV.

secured salvation, and provided a means of escape from the pains of purgatory, relatives often were compelled to pay exorbitant fees, or else be tormented by the thought that they had abandoned their loved ones to unnecessary suffering. Many medieval councils tried to cope with these evils, but in vain. They were inherent in the system which had turned a sacrament of healing into a preparation for death.

These, then, were the beliefs and customs with which the reformers were faced. Unction stood outside their definition of a sacrament. It had no sign which could be reasonably attributed to our Lord. The grace which it was supposed to convey was not that indicated by the Form which accompanied its administration. Clearly it had undergone great changes in the course of time. Even if some authority for it existed in the epistle of St James, the service with which they were familiar was, at best, "a corrupt following", and even St James afforded no justification for the popular belief that a sinner, who might be unconscious, could by a bodily anointing escape judgement. They knew that our Lord had commanded his ministers to "heal the sick". But unction had ceased to be a method of healing. The benefits which it pretended to bestow were much more certainly given through penance and communion. In the form with which they were familiar, extreme unction was indefensible—so they swept it away. But they did not denounce it as wrong.

Nothing was put into the Prayer Book calculated to make its restoration difficult. If the Church of England should wish to restore unction there would be nothing to unsay. As a matter of fact some of the provinces of the Anglican Communion have already restored it with the original aim of healing the body. The bishops of the Church of India, Burma, and Ceylon in the Prefatory Statement of their Constitution and Canons actually listed it among the things which they inherited from the Church of England and purposed to maintain. Some bishops in England regularly bless oil every Maundy Thursday for use in cases of sickness. Lambeth conferences have noted these facts and approved them. They are not inconsistent in any way with the principles declared in the Prayer Book.

The reformers knew that the Church has a duty to perform for the sick. To fulfil this they drew up a new service of Visitation. Why they replaced the old one, which was wholly admirable, is hard to understand. Possibly it was because the old one looked forward confidently to recovery, and they wanted to combine hope with preparation for death. Whatever their aim they produced a service which few can find adequate, and which would seem seldom, if ever, to be used in its entirety. The place of the admirably chosen psalms and lessons of the old service has been replaced by long-winded exhortations and, if the truth must be told, an unhelpful psalm. The very ancient laying-on of the priest's hands is omitted. The service is the poorest in the Prayer Book. But however much we may condemn the reformers for their foolishness in not simply translating the old service for the sick, and producing a new one for the dying, nevertheless we are bound to acknowledge that they did make provision for the essentials of Catholic care for the sick. Their new service orders the priest to test the patient's faith, to inquire into his relations with others and to endeavour to lead him to charity and concord with all men, to help him make such provision as he can for his dependants and for the needy, to help him to probe his conscience if it is uneasy, to move him to make his confession, to absolve him after such confession, and to give him Holy Communion. All the Catholic things are there, except anointing and the laying-on of the priest's hand.

A word is necessary about the communion of the sick because here also there was an innovation. This was not in doctrine. Our Lord's Body and Blood were still to be administered to them, and there was no minimizing of the importance of the Viaticum. From very early times the sick had been communicated with the reserved sacrament and it had been forbidden to celebrate Holy Communion in a private house. There had been well-known exceptions to these rules, one of the most famous being that of St Dunstan, who had Mass celebrated at his bedside while he lay dying, and so received the Viaticum. The reformers did not forbid reservation for the sick, and it is certain that in some places continuous reservation was practised without hindrance for many years after the break with Rome.

Article XXVIII does not forbid reservation. It simply states the undeniable fact that our Lord did not command it. The rubric at the end of the Communion Service states that "If any of the Bread and Wine remain unconsecrated, the Curate shall have it to his own use: but if any remain of that which was consecrated, it shall not be carried out of the church, but the Priest . . . shall immediately after the Blessing, reverently eat and drink the same." This was inserted in 1662, not to forbid reservation, but to prohibit the sacrilegious custom of some of the Puritans, who treated what remained of the Blessed Sacrament as ordinary food. But reservation for the sick was gradually replaced by the custom of the earliest ages in which the Blessed Sacrament was carried to them after the parish communion. Provision for this was made in the First Prayer Book, and continued in the second, wherein the priest was ordered to "minister" Holy Communion to the sick. "Minister" in current usage always meant "communicate", not "consecrate", therefore "to minister" the Blessed Sacrament to the sick involved carrying it to them from the parish altar. When it was difficult to do this the reformers authorized celebrations in private houses. The "proper" for the Communion of the Sick was not inserted in the Prayer Book until 1662.

When our reformers gave permission to celebrate in private houses they undoubtedly departed from custom, for which the East is entitled to blame us, for the Orthodox have maintained the principle that Mass may be celebrated only in a consecrated church. But the Pope sometimes grants dispensations to missionaries and old priests allowing them to celebrate in their houses. Rome therefore has abandoned the strict rule and "what Rome condones, let not Rome condemn" would seem to be a just maxim. The ancient canon which orders the parish priest to reserve for the sake of the sick and dying has never been repealed.

It is submitted that the worst that can be said of the action of our reformers in this sphere of the Church's ministration is that they missed a great opportunity. They might have restored the custom of the primitive Church, to which they so often appealed. But it is not just to blame them for what they did, in view of the confusion which surrounded the whole subject, and the very real abuses which had accumulated around it. Perhaps it was right for them to strike at the root of the evils with which they were faced by abandoning practices which had been abused, in such a way that when danger was passed the Church of England could recover sacramental healing according to the use of the undivided Church. But, surely, it is impossible to maintain that a Church, which made such careful provision for the spiritual health of the sick and dying as the Church of England did, broke away from the unity of Christ's Body by its action in this matter.

CHAPTER 15

THE LIFE AFTER DEATH

IT CANNOT be denied that at the Reformation the Church of England took up a position, with regard to beliefs about the life after death, and with practices concerning the departed, which differed considerably, both doctrinally and devotionally, from that which had been customary for many centuries in both East and West. Our reformers reacted violently against the popular beliefs and practices of their day. But why did they do so? Their actions were not necessarily wrong. Were the things which they disliked truly Catholic? Would our Lord and his apostles and the primitive Church have agreed with them, or with their opponents? These questions are by no means easy to answer.

Fortified by our Lord's declaration that "all live to God", the Christian Church took over the doctrine of the Pharisees that there are no dead. Death is an event, not a state. It is something which happens to the body. The body corrupts and disintegrates. But the spirit and soul continue to live. Death separates bodies, but it does not divide at the higher level of the spirit, and especially is that true in the Church. This is the Body of Christ. It is one body, made up of members, some of whom live in the flesh, whilst others have passed beyond the veil, whither the Head of the Church has gone before. The phrase "falling asleep", which occurs so frequently in the New Testament, as a synonym for death, refers to the body only. This is very clear in the story of our Lord's death. "He gave up the ghost." His personality departed from his body, and his body died. But he himself, his spirit, remained alive. He went and "preached to the spirits in prison".[1] To render this mission fruitful it was necessary that they also were alive and conscious.

But what is the lot of the departed? Where are they? There are many indications in the New Testament that they are assembled

[1] 1 Pet. 3.19.

in at least two companies—that of the saints and that of the faithful
departed. There are indications of a third, those who are awaiting
the "resurrection of damnation". To these the Middle Ages added
a fourth, which contained the souls of those who, although they
had lived in accordance with the highest standards they knew, had
nevertheless been ignorant of the Light of Christ. He had said
"no man cometh to the Father, but by me"[1] and "except a man
be born of water and of the Spirit he cannot enter into the
kingdom of God".[2] In consequence the unbaptized could not be
in Heaven. But the Christian conscience revolted from the thought
that they were automatically condemned to perdition. Especially
was it impossible to hold that infants who died unbaptized,
obviously through no fault of their own, could be "lost". So the
custom arose of thinking about such souls as being in a place which
came to be called Limbo. It was taught that those in it were as
happy as their natures allowed, but that their condition fell short
of the glory of the Beatific Vision. This was a Western speculation,
which never found favour in the East. The Prayer Book says
nothing at all about it, preferring to leave all the unbaptized
to the uncovenanted mercies of the God of love. Apparently
we are free to believe in Limbo, if we care to do so. The
Church of England does not deny that in the house of the
Heavenly Father there "are many mansions",[3] or that these
words of our Lord may well mean that there are variations of
blessedness.

The saints are in Heaven. The Apocalypse provides sufficient
evidence for this. It tells us of the Elders, who worship before
the Throne:[4] of the thousands of the tribes of Israel who were
sealed;[5] of the multitude "which no man could number"[6] that
stands before the Lamb; of the virgins, who follow him "whither-
soever he goeth";[7] of the faithful who have come "out of great
tribulation, and washed their robes, and made them white in the
blood of the Lamb", and now stand "before the throne of God,
and serve him day and night".[8] In the Epistle to the Hebrews we
are told that the saints are "a great cloud of witnesses"[9] in the

[1] John 14.6.   [2] John 3.5.   [3] John 14.2.
[4] Rev. 4.4; 5.14.   [5] Rev. 7.4.   [6] Rev. 7.9.
[7] Rev. 14.4.   [8] Rev. 7.14,15.   [9] Heb. 12.1.

heavenly places who compass us about, and that "just men made perfect"[1] are in heavenly Zion.

That the saints are still interested in us can be deduced from the fact that at the Transfiguration Moses and Elias returned to earth to talk with our Lord about his coming passion.[2] In the parable of Dives and Lazarus we are told that Dives was still concerned with the well-being of his brethren.[3] In the passage in the Epistle to the Hebrews, which has already been quoted, the saints are presented to us as spectators, sitting around an arena, interested in the victory of the athletes, because "they without us should not be made perfect".[4]

Because of this vital interest in us the saints pray for us. Bishop Gibson says that "this was certainly the belief of the Jews, as is shown by more than one passage", and he goes on to quote 2 Macc. 15. 12–14: "Onias, who had been high priest, holding up his hands, prayed for the whole body of the Jews. This done, there appeared a man with grey hairs, and exceeding glorious, who was of wonderful excellency and majesty. Then Onias answered, saying, This is a man of the brethren, who prayeth much for the people, and for the holy city, to wit, Jeremias, the prophet of God." Jeremiah had been long dead. This belief that the saints pray for us was taken over by the Christian Church and was never a subject of controversy amongst Catholics. Those who are "without fault before the throne of God"[5] pray for their brethren on earth, who although sinners, are nevertheless one with them in the Body of Christ.

But not all who die are saints. Of how few could it be truthfully said that, like St Paul, they had fought the fight, finished the course and kept the faith, so that there was laid up for them a crown of righteousness? It may be that few are wholly evil. On the other hand is it not certain that very few can be wholly good? What, then, is the dwelling place of those who, though stained by sin, have not denied God; who, although they have often been overcome by temptation, have fought against it; who, although they have often failed, have nevertheless struggled on towards

---

[1] Heb. 12.23.   [2] Luke 9.30,31.   [3] Luke 16.28.
[4] Heb. 11.40. Although the term "witness" means "witness to truth", nevertheless the general picture of an arena suggests "spectators".
[5] Rev. 14.5.

God? The New Testament has many indications that they form a company whose lot is joy or suffering in proportion to their deserts. They are not yet in Heaven, but they are being made fit to enter it. Death does not change automatically a sinful man into a sinless one. We carry into the life beyond the grave the same personalities, the same characters, with their weaknesses and their strength, that are ours when we die. Ordinary souls, therefore, cannot be in Heaven. Where, then, are they?

The Church's answer is that they are in a place of waiting, where they are being prepared for the Beatific Vision. This place is called both Paradise and purgatory. These are not two places, but one and the same, looked at from different points of view. From one aspect, the place of waiting is the Garden of God, for it involves peace after war, rest after toil, refreshment after labour, light after the darkness of this world. The souls there no longer sin, temptation does not allure them, they no longer grope their way through uncertainties. Theirs is the assurance of eventual perfection. Therefore they are in "Paradise",[1] in "Abraham's bosom".[2] But the companionship of Abraham must fall far short of the realized presence of God. All the faults in the characters of the holy souls must be purged away before they can attain that perfection of "holiness without which no man shall see the Lord".[3] They have to grow in their understanding of the perfect love of God and in the many ways they have injured it. They have to realize how the majesty of him who is Almighty has been insulted, and slighted and injured by their human wilfulness. They have to learn how the evil, which they have done on earth, has influenced and harmed the souls of others. To learn these things must involve suffering. Therefore the place of waiting is purgatory, as well as Paradise. And these two are one. The penitent thief to whom it was promised that he should spend the night of his death with his Saviour "in Paradise" was nevertheless "in prison", for it was there that, as St Peter tells us,[4] our Lord's soul passed.

For the holy souls the Church has prayed from the very beginning. Indeed, Christians of the first generation did a much stranger thing than pray for their dead—they even "baptized for the

---

[1] Luke 23.43.   [2] Luke 16.22.
[3] Heb. 12.14.   [4] 1 Pet. 3.19.

dead".[1] The earliest Christian monuments bear such inscriptions as "grant him peace". The practice was in fact inherited from the Jews. Long before our Lord's time sacrifices were regularly offered in the Temple for the dead. One quotation must suffice to prove the custom. In 2 Maccabees 12, we are told how, after a battle, the great leader, Judas Maccabeus made a collection throughout his army and sent the money to Jerusalem to pay for a sin offering for the dead, "doing therein very well and honestly . . . for if he had not hoped that they which were slain should have risen again, it had been vain and superfluous to pray for the dead. . . . But in that he perceived that there was great favour laid up for those that died godly, it was a holy and good thought. Whereupon he made a reconciliation for the dead, that they might be delivered from sin."

These points, therefore, can be said to be Catholic and, indeed, to fulfil the Anglican test of orthodoxy, in that they can be proved from Scripture. The souls of the departed are all alive to God. They are conscious and they are still interested in their brethren on earth. The saints in glory aid us by praying for us. We can help the souls, who are not yet made perfect, by our prayers. The Communion of Saints is a reality and the Body of Christ is a unity.

That was as much as the Church taught in the first centuries of its life, and the Prayer Book enshrines all the foregoing principles. The unity of the whole Body of Christ is clearly expressed in the collect for All Saints' Day: "God, who hast knit together thine elect in one communion and *fellowship*." There is a fellowship in Christ, which embraces, not only those members who are still in the flesh, but also those who have passed beyond the veil. We believe in the Communion of Saints. Nevertheless something has gone. The practices, which were founded upon this doctrine, of asking for the prayers of the saints and of praying for the departed were cut out of the Prayer Book.

The reformers succeeded in banishing almost entirely the thought of the saints and the departed first from "official", and then from popular, religion, and it cannot be denied that such was their intention. But why? Because around the simple faith and practice of the primitive Church there had grown up a host of

[1] 1 Cor. 15.29.

dark beliefs and superstitious practices. It is probable that even in the earliest ages, when, as the evidence of the Liturgies proves, the Church besought God to allow its members on earth to benefit through the prayers of the saints, popular devotion went much further. Inscriptions on tombs in the catacombs often invoke the departed directly—"glorious martyr, pray for us". But the doctors of the Church have usually shown some doubt about the legitimacy of addressing the departed directly. As late as the twelfth century Peter Lombard, who is honoured as a "Doctor", wrote "it is not incredible that the souls of the saints do in the contemplation [of God] understand the things which are done in this world";[1] "not incredible" cannot be described as an enthusiastic foundation for invocation. Even as late as the sixteenth century Cardinal Cajetan could state that "we have no certain knowledge as to whether the saints are aware of our prayers, though we piously believe it".[2] These illustrations could be multiplied many times from the writings of men who, even from the Roman point of view, were unquestionably orthodox. They prove that the Catholic Church until the late Middle Ages felt some hesitation, officially, about the practice of directly invoking the saints. But what the Council of Trent called the "vulgar people" have had no doubt at all. Popular devotion to the saints grew until it became almost the whole of religion, and all but hid the face of God and the love of his Son. Although direct invocations of the saints never found a place in Western liturgies, they were introduced into private prayers very early, and by the eighth century they were inserted into litanies. The most astonishing feature in this development of popular religion was the cultus of our Lady. She gradually assumed all the loving characteristics of her Son, who came to be regarded as a stern and hard judge, rather than as a redeemer. "Jesus has saved his thousands, but Mary her tens of thousands." In popular estimation the shortest cut to the satisfaction of some desire was to enlist the aid of our Lady, or some of the saints, whose prayers to God were powerful. It was not only the ignorant who felt in this way. St Bonaventura could pray, "O Empress and most kind Lady, by the authority of a mother, *command* thy Son".[3]

[1] Quoted by Gibson, *XXXIX Articles.*   [2] Quoted ibid.
[3] Gibson, ibid.

Erasmus, whose orthodoxy was unimpeachable, and who was a very close friend of St Thomas More, wrote, "I call it superstition when all things are asked of the saints as if Christ were dead; or when we implore the aid of the saints with the idea that they are more easily entreated than God; or when we seek some particular thing from each, as if St Catherine could bestow what St Barbara could not; or when we call upon them, not as intercessors, but as authors of the good things which God grants us."[1] All these customs, which Erasmus calls "monstrous superstitions" were rife in the later Middle Ages. It is not surprising that our reformers reacted violently against them. But Article XXII, which condemns the Romish doctrine of the invocation of saints, does not condemn the official Roman Catholic doctrine. The decrees of the Council of Trent on the subject were not promulgated until after the Article had been approved. When at last the Tridentine fathers published their decree it bore "striking testimony to the existence of the errors which had called forth the vigorous protest of our own reformers".[1]

The term "Romish" demands some consideration. The Article was drawn up first in the reign of Edward VI. What was then condemned was "the doctrine of the Schoolmen", that is to say the whole body of medieval teaching on the subject. This would have barred every simple petition for the prayers of any saint. In Elizabeth's reign the word was changed deliberately to "Romish". The effect of this was to "make the Article condemn a *present* current form of teaching, rather than the formal system of doctors, whose day was past".[2] "Romish" does not mean the official teaching of the Roman Church but a perversion of it, the same perversion, in fact, which the Council of Trent was to condemn. It is important to emphasize the fact that not only did our reformers never condemn the foundation doctrines on which popular practice was based, but they did not immediately abandon all invocations. Some were retained, deliberately, in the First Prayer Book and it was officially declared in the Second that no condemnation was intended of the doctrines of the former Book, which was "a very godly order . . . agreeable to the Word of God and the primitive Church". The Church of England therefore

[1] Gibson, *XXXIX Articles.*   [2] Gibson, ibid.

9

acknowledges the legitimacy of the "ora pro nobis", even if it does not now make use of it in its liturgical services.

The Church of England adopted much the same negative position with regard to purgatory and the faithful departed. It is quite certain that in the later Middle Ages very many scandalous practices and grave superstitions had grown up around death. It was commonly believed that the souls in purgatory suffered actual physical torment, and the exploitation of the love and pity of the bereaved provided many clergy with a profitable source of income. The whole system was rotten with abuses, and it is not surprising that the reaction against it was violent. Even the Council of Trent acknowledged that imagination had run riot and that reforms were badly needed. The decree of the Council states simply

there is a Purgatory and the souls there retained are relieved by the suffrages of the faithful, but chiefly by the acceptable sacrifice of the altar . . . among the uneducated vulgar, let the more difficult and subtle questions, and those which tend not to edification, and seldom contribute aught to piety, be kept back from popular discourses. Neither let them suffer the public mention and treatment of uncertain points, or such as look like falsehood. But those things which tend to a certain kind of curiosity or superstition, or which savour of filthy lucre, let them prohibit as scandals and stumbling blocks of the faithful.[1]

It is quite obvious that the Council realized that there was something very wrong with popular devotion. "Uneducated vulgar", "subtle questions", "uncertain points", "like falsehood", "curiosity or superstition", "filthy lucre", "scandals and stumbling blocks", here is a regular barrage of hard words. Is it surprising that if the fathers of Trent could use such language our English reformers were somewhat violent also? They did condemn the "Romish" abuses which Trent condemned, but they did not deny the simple doctrine that there is a purgatory, nor did they condemn prayers for the departed. They never promulgated any heretical doctrine about the future life. They pruned popular custom in a drastic manner, but there is nothing positive in their statements which a Catholic is bound to contradict. In consequence, when once the violence of the first reforming generation had spent itself, there began a steady movement of recovery of truly Catholic

[1] Session XXV, Dec. 1563.

faith and practice. As early as the reign of James I, Bishop Andrewes was asserting that the Church of England had never condemned the doctrine of purgatory and that it was lawful for Churchmen to hold it. In 1662 a somewhat vague supplication for the departed was inserted into the prayer for the Church Militant, and the proposed Book of 1928 contained open intercession for them. The facts are that grave abuses led to violent reaction, but as soon as the dangers of abuse had passed away, there began a steady movement back to Catholic practice.

But it cannot be denied that in all that concerns the saints and the faithful departed the Reformation produced something like a revolution in popular religion. Thoughts and practices, which had been central, faded away completely. Ordinary folk came to believe that the dead either passed straight to Heaven, or were sleeping until the Day of Judgement. Purgatory was a fond invention. The departed had passed beyond human reach. Heaven was a far away place and its inhabitants could not still be interested in the doings of the world, nor could they be benefited by prayers. The "Communion of Saints" lost all meaning. As the irreligion which sprang from the Renaissance spread, and as it gained strength from materialistic philosophy and science, this world became more and more important. Men rediscovered the point of view of the Sadducees. *This* was the real world. Heaven was a vague "kingdom of fairies in the dark",[1] a pious hope, a wishful thought. It was this life which mattered. The world to come, which had been the great aim and inspiration of life ceased to inspire. That change took place and it was greatly helped by the work of the reformers. They had no intention of doing any such thing but, by removing from popular devotion the practices which fostered thought about the future life, they created a vacuum which the devil speedily filled with temporal interests. By encouraging this revolution did they sever the Church of England from the Catholic Church?

Our reformers put away practices which were most certainly Catholic, in that they belonged to both East and West and had been in popular use from very early times. Nevertheless this act, even if it had not been dictated by the seriousness of the abuses

[1] Hobbes.

which occasioned it, could not have caused a breach of Catholic unity—unless the abandoned practices were necessary to salvation. Are they? It can be granted that they are extremely useful and that some are very beautiful—it can even be accepted that our reformers were wrong when they jettisoned them—but all those things miss the point. That is, are they part of the essential practice of the Church, so that any responsible person could maintain that a man who made use of all the covenanted means of grace and humbly tried to be a faithful Christian, was in danger of forfeiting eternal life because, for example, he did not ask for the prayers of our Lady, or pray for the repose of the soul of his dead mother? Can we say that? We may feel that the case for both invoking the saints and praying for the dead is so very strong, because of universal custom, that it is dangerous to neglect them. But can we say that anyone who does so thereby cuts himself off from Christ? Everyone with any knowledge of the way in which these practices developed, is forced to answer such questions by a decided negative. It is simply not thinkable that St Paul, or the pre-Nicene fathers, would have excommunicated anyone because they would neither ask for the prayers of the saints, nor pray for the repose of the faithful departed. That being so, the Church of England cannot possibly have broken away from the unity of the Church when, under great provocation, it abandoned for a time customs which are not essential to the Catholic life.

CHAPTER 16

THE ROYAL VERSUS THE PAPAL SUPREMACY

WHEN our reformers had done their work, Englishmen were breathing a different spiritual atmosphere from that which had prevailed in the later Middle Ages. That cannot be denied. From the time of the Council of Whitby (664) the Church of England had been an integral part of the Western Church, but after the Reformation it stood alone. When it began the final authority in religion had been the Pope. After the Reformation his place had been taken by a lay sovereign; first the King, and later, as is still the case, by Parliament. Sometimes an attempt is made to blur the issue by suggesting that the survival of the Church's own parliament, Convocation, really left the direction of spiritual matters in the hands of the Church. That is not strictly true. Sir Thomas More knew as much about Convocation as we do, and he died because, as he put it, "a lay sovereign cannot be head of the spirituality". From the time of Henry VIII's breach with the Papacy effective power was in the hands of the sovereign. Archbishop Langton led the barons who forced King John to sign Magna Charta, which in its first clause promised freedom from royal control to the Church of England. Henry VIII figuratively tore up that scrap of paper. He destroyed in England the ideal of the Church as dominant in the world, with the Pope as the Vicar of Christ dictating to secular rulers, Even the great vision of an *imperium in imperio* which Hildebrand had seen faded completely away. Its place was taken by the idea of the autonomous State, with its lay sovereign supreme ruler of all in his dominions, the fountain of ecclesiastical honour as well as civil, laying down the law for Church as well as State, permitting no appeal to any higher earthly authority. That revolution took place. From the first the action was defended on the ground that the anointed King was God's viceregent. A secular national sovereign took the place of an international spiritual one.

The terms "secular" and "spiritual" are convenient, but they are very inaccurate. The Popes, in some aspects, were as obviously temporal sovereigns as any Emperor or King. On the other hand the King of England always claimed to be a spiritual sovereign, in that he ruled by the will of God. His claim was based on hereditary succession, not on the will of Parliament, or because of the blessing of the Church. State and Church merely recognized a right which had already been conferred by God. Roman controversialists seldom do justice to the fact that the reformers believed that the monarchy was a divine institution. How did the idea arise?

In a sense it did not arise at all. A belief, which had always been present in civilization, became intensified.

When the Church moved out to the conquest of the world the Emperor was an absolute monarch, and the High Priest of the empire. There could be no superior channel of revelation. Then, with the death of Augustus, the process began of deifying the departed sovereign, and very soon he began to be treated as God and worshipped as such immediately he became Emperor. Constantine inaugurated an era of toleration, and Christianity soon became the dominant religion of the empire, but the Emperors did not cease to be supreme over all persons and causes just because they became Christians.

Constantine divided the empire for administrative purposes into East and West, and although there were usually two Emperors, in theory the empire was one. As a matter of fact the two halves began almost at once to draw apart and the history of the monarchy in each was different. In the East the Emperor was vested in robes, which though secular in origin, quickly assumed a symbolic and ecclesiastical significance. He was counted amongst the clergy and allowed to enter the sanctuary, to kiss the altar, and to handle the Host. As late as 729 he claimed to be "Emperor and Priest", and one of the charges brought against some heretics was that they refused to recognize his spiritual authority. Justinian the Great (527) was hailed as Priest-King, and it was his bishop that first gave expression to the theory, later to be proclaimed by William I, Henry II, and Henry VIII, "nothing should happen in the Church against the command and will of the Emperor".[1] The

1 Baynes, *Byzantine Empire.*

Emperor was very definitely the supreme lawgiver of the Church. He alone could summon a council and Constantine, whilst still unbaptized, presided at the Council of Nicea. At later Councils, when the Emperor was not present in person his lay commissioners presided, and no conclusions of a Council became law, or had any force, until they had received imperial approval. "In time these Councils appeared dangerously democratic, and the autocrat of Constantinople defined the dogmas of the Church by imperial edict."[1] Patriarchs and bishops may be said to have held office by the Emperor's will, for he deposed them when he thought fit. Although many ecclesiastics opposed various manifestations of imperial policy no dispute arose about its theory. This remained the position in the Eastern empire until it was destroyed by the Mohammedans, and it was continued in the greatest daughter Church of Constantinople, Russia. The Tsars inherited the absolutism of the Emperors, ruling Church and State alike until the Bolshevik revolution.

But even in the East, there was some difference between the authority of the Pagan and Christian emperors. The Church inherited from the Jews the belief in the absolute overruling sovereignty of God, "by whose power kings reign".[2] The Christian rulers, although their power was not limited by any human authority, were nevertheless the subjects of the King of Kings. They were not gods, like the pagan Emperors. Because that was so, law was not just what they decreed. It was what God had decreed and they were morally bound to rule in accordance with his will. Even the greatest of the Eastern Emperors recognized the obligation, and this had very important consequences. These may be illustrated by a story. When Theodosius (379), one of the strongest of the Emperors, received news of a riot in Thessalonica, in which many soldiers had been killed, he flew into a rage. Declaring that the whole town was responsible, he ordered a massacre of its inhabitants. In pagan times nothing could have been done. A Tiberius could no more have been called to account than Jupiter. But St Ambrose, the Bishop of Milan, which was at that period the most important city in the West, excommunicated Theodosius, until he acknowledged that he had been guilty of the sin of murder,

[1] Ibid.   [2] Prov. 8.15.

and had done penance. Be it noted that St Ambrose acted without any reference to the Pope. Two facts stand out clearly—the idea of law as the will of God, not merely that of an earthly sovereign, and, secondly, the appearance of a Churchman as the prophet, who declares the will of God to an earthly sovereign and imposes punishment upon him. In that aspect the Churchman is the superior of the Emperor. The incident clearly shows how, by the acceptance of Christianity, the Emperors accepted also the idea that their sovereignty was limited by God's law.

But who is to interpret that law? In the East it was, very largely, the Emperor who did so, although there were spirited protests from time to time. An historic case is that of St Athanasius, who went into exile five times rather than accept the faith imposed by the Emperor, even when it was endorsed by the great majority of his bishops. But, as we have seen, usually the Emperor ruled as God's viceregent and his authority, inherited from his pagan predecessors, was unchallenged. It was the Emperor who was pre-eminently the representative of God on earth.

The history of the West differed very greatly from that of the East. The barbarian tribes, Goths, Vandals, Huns, Franks, Angles, and Saxons overran the empire until centralized government from Rome became a thing of the past. It ceased in Britain in 410, in France about 450, and in Spain a little later. By 493 Theodore the Goth was the sole ruler of Italy, Romulus Augustulus, the last Western Emperor, having abdicated in 476. Although each of these various peoples had some kind of internal cohesion, their organization was tribal. Even within each "nation" clan feuds and violence were endemic, and there were truces in the perpetual civil wars only when some ruffian chieftain made himself strong enough to be feared by his neighbours and to be obeyed in his own territory. These barbarian rulers would have known no law, save their own wills, if it had not been for one fact—they had become Christians.

The Church survived the barbaric deluge with its organization intact. All other civilized governments collapsed. As the savage chieftains snatched power from the feeble hands of lay officials, the unhappy inhabitants of towns and villages turned to their bishops for protection and justice. That they were often able to

help their flocks was due to the fears which their office inspired
in the minds of the conquerors. Almost all the dominating figures
of the Dark Ages are Churchmen. In 452 it was the Pope, Leo I,
not the civil magistrate, who went out to meet Alaric and his Huns
and so overawe them that they abandoned their intention of
sacking Rome. According to tradition it was the bishop, St
Germain, and St Geneviève, who saved Paris from the Franks.
When some secular sovereign attains greatness usually there is to
be discerned behind him some clerical scholar or statesman
guiding and supporting him. But neither the Popes nor the bishops
usurped the authority of the State. When they found the thrones
of Caesar and his viceroys vacant, and sat on them, it was wholly
for the good of both Church and people that they did so. It was
right that they should use their authority to tide over an inter-
regnum. But was it right that spiritual persons should cling to
secular power, and its "spoils", after secular authority had been
restored?

The Roman Catholic Argument from Scripture

Obviously, in such circumstances, the old theory of the supreme
imperial viceregent of God was untenable. But since man cannot
live by the bread of a *fait accompli* alone, but must justify it in
some way to his conscience, during all the period in which the
Church was keeping alive the idea of law and order, a theory of
papal jurisdiction was being built up to explain the fact. From the
beginning of the Christian era men had looked to Rome as the
seat of government and the final court of appeal in all secular
matters. St Paul, fearing the unjust judgement of a subordinate
official, claimed the right of every Roman citizen and appealed
to Caesar. From the distinctively Christian point of view, Rome
was the city where both the Apostle to the Hebrews and the
Apostle to the Gentiles had worked and which they had sanctified
by the blood of their martyrdoms. It was natural that the voice of
their successors should be heard with the greatest respect. There
was no other apostolic see in the West to diminish the prestige of
the bishops, whose seats were in the capital of the world. Thus
the custom of appealing to the Pope grew up naturally and without

challenge, so far as the West was concerned. The East also listened with deep respect to the voice of Rome, although, for the most part, definite appeals came from defeated minorities. When it was desired to justify this situation, the way was clear. Was not the Pope the successor of St Peter and therefore the inheritor of the authority symbolized by the gift of the keys of the Kingdom of Heaven? Did not our Lord promise to build his Church on the rock that was Peter? The situation is one which occurs again and again in history. It is the result of what may be called "gradualness". Precedent is built upon precedent until at last a position is reached which is quite new. It is then justified by a novel interpretation of the original facts. The point about the power of binding and loosing was that it was *not* bestowed upon St Peter when our Lord spoke the words recorded in Matthew 16. 15–19. Read them—they are a promise to do something in the future: "To thee I *will* give the keys of the kingdom of heaven." When was the promise fulfilled? There is no record at all, except one when St Peter was with the other apostles. There was nothing in the promise to suggest that St Peter *alone* was to receive the authority symbolized by the keys, and as a matter of fact he was associated with others when our Lord "breathed on them and said unto them Receive ye the Holy Ghost: whosoever sins ye remit, they are remitted unto them, and whosoever sins ye retain, they are retained".[1] Secondly, the words "this rock" do not refer to St Peter at all, but to the faith in the Incarnation which he had just professed. Here is the whole passage in full. Our Lord asked his disciples (Peter, James, and John),

But whom say ye that I am? And Simon Peter answered and said, Thou art the Christ, the Son of the living God. And Jesus answered and said unto him, Blessed art thou, Simon Bar-Jona: for flesh and blood hath not revealed it unto thee, but my Father which is in heaven. And I say also unto thee, That thou art Peter, and upon this rock I will build my church; and the gates of hell shall not prevail against it. And I will give to thee the keys of the kingdom of heaven: and whatsoever thou shalt bind on earth shall be bound in heaven and whatsoever thou shalt loose on earth shall be loosed in heaven. Then charged he his disciples that they should tell no man that he was Jesus the Christ.

It was the statement that our Lord was the Christ, the Son of

[1] John 20.22.

God[1] which brought St Peter his blessing, and the whole passage ends on the same note. Because St Peter confessed his faith in the Incarnation, our Lord called him a Rock-man. But the rock on which the Church is to be built is the fact of the Incarnation— "Thou art the Christ, the Son of the living God." Clearly that was what St Paul believed. He wrote "other foundation can no man lay than that is laid, which is Jesus Christ".[2] St Peter himself says the same thing: "The Lord is gracious. To whom coming, as unto a living stone . . . ye also, as living stones, are built up a spiritual house. . . . Wherefore also it is contained in Scripture, Behold, I lay in Sion a chief corner stone, elect, precious: and he that believeth on him shall not be confounded."[3] This passage is particularly important because it echoes the words said by our Lord to St Peter himself, Not only himself, but all the faithful are Peters, "living stones". *The* Stone, the stone on which the whole building of the Church depends, is our Lord. By no stretch of imagination can St Peter's words be twisted so that they can be made to convey the doctrine that "the rock" on which the Church is built is anything but our Lord himself. This interpretation of our Lord's words to St Peter is supported by the fact that it is still to be found in the Roman Missal. However difficult it may be for the Roman controversialists to explain, the collect for the vigil of the feast of SS. Peter and Paul states that God has firmly established his Church "as on a rock, on the apostolic confession".

It is necessary to glance very quickly at the other texts by which the papal claims have been justified. There are only two. They are Luke 22. 31–2, and John 21. 15–17. The first is "And the Lord said, Simon, Simon, behold, Satan hath desired to have you, that he may sift you as wheat: but I have prayed for thee, that thy faith fail not: and when thou art converted, strengthen thy brethren." It is difficult to understand how anyone can make more of this than that it is a prophecy that St Peter is to undergo some especially painful temptation, as he did when he denied his master. He was told that his experience was to be turned to good, so that because of it he was to "strengthen" his brethren. There is no suggestion at all that he was to exercise any especial authority. The fact that "strengthen" is interpreted to mean that he was to

[1] See Appendix C.   [2] I Cor. 3.11.   [3] I Pet. 2.3–6.

"supervise" them shows to what straits the supporters of the papal claim are reduced in order to justify their position.

There are some judgements about St Peter which we can make without hesitation. He was what is called a "born leader of men". He was the man whose defection would have most injured the witness of the apostles. Therefore he must have had a very important place in God's plan. But he was also a very humble man. There is an ancient tradition, which there is no reason to disbelieve, that at his martyrdom he begged to be crucified head downwards because, on account of his denial, he had rendered himself unworthy to suffer in exactly the same way that his master had suffered. We do not need this story, however, to assure us of his humility. The earliest record about such things tells us that St Mark's gospel is actually the teaching which St Peter gave to his converts, so that it is in reality the Gospel according to St Peter. In that gospel there is recorded everything to St Peter's discredit —for example, the story of the denial is told with an emphasis, and with a wealth of detail, that are absent from the other gospels. On the other hand his great confession of faith and the blessing and promise which it won are omitted. These facts speak of perfect humility. St Peter will relate anything to his discredit and be silent about a matter which is to his credit. But this great and humble leader had denied our Lord three times. How could he be assured that he was forgiven? How could he be induced to use his great gifts in the service of his master and not be inhibited by the thought of his failure? Surely one way would be for him to receive a special commission. That is exactly what he did.

Jesus saith to Simon Peter, Simon, son of Jonas, lovest thou me . . .? He saith unto him, Yea, Lord; thou knowest that I love thee. He saith unto him, Feed my lambs. He saith unto him again the second time, Simon, son of Jonas, lovest thou me? He saith unto him, Yea, Lord; thou knowest that I love thee. He saith unto him, Feed my sheep. He saith unto him the third time, Simon, son of Jonas, lovest thou me? Peter was grieved because he said unto him the third time, Lovest thou me? And he said unto him, Lord, thou knowest all things; thou knowest that I love thee. Jesus saith unto him, Feed my sheep.[1]

"Here", say the Roman controversialists, "we have a clear grant of universal jurisdiction to St Peter. In a very especial way he is to

[1] John 21.15.

feed the lambs and sheep of Christ." But the passage means nothing of the sort. When our Lord desired to convey authority he did so in unmistakable terms: "As my Father hath sent me, even so send I you." This passage conveys no grant of authority. It is a threefold absolution for a threefold denial. "Peter was grieved because he said unto him the *third* time, Lovest thou me?" Of course he was, because the threefold probe was intended to remind him clearly of the threefold failure. "Thou knowest all things. Thou knowest that I denied thrice, but thou knowest that in spite of my cowardice, I really do love thee." That is the sentiment conveyed by the text, and our Lord's reiterated commission was intended to make St Peter absolutely certain of forgiveness for the past, and of our Lord's continued trust in him. Is it not as certain as such a matter can well be, that only by some such renewal of his commission could a man as humble as St Peter have been induced to throw his whole weight into the apostolic task of witness?

If the Roman interpretations of these Petrine texts were true then we should expect to find some indications in the other books of the New Testament that they were accepted by the Church of the apostolic age as in some measure setting St Peter above his fellow apostles. There is not one scrap of evidence for this. When the Church was faced with its first vital decision, a decision which involved a policy which made the Church truly universal, but which might have left it for ever a sect of Judaism, the apostles met in Council at Jerusalem. If it had been believed that in some way our Lord had appointed St Peter the Head of the Apostolic College, that he, in fact, was the Vicar of Christ, is there any doubt that he would have presided at the meeting? He did make a very important speech. But the "president" of the Council, the man who summed up the arguments and gave the first vote "my sentence is", which sentence became the official direction to the Gentiles, was not St Peter, but St James.[1]

From the freedom which this decision gave to the Gentiles, St Peter afterwards declined. It seems that pressure was put upon him by the judaizing party, and he began to try to make Gentile converts keep the Old Testament law. In consequence there arose

[1] Acts 15.3.

a controversy between him and St Paul. In the course of this St Paul says, "I withstood him to the face, because he was to be blamed".[1] In this contention St Peter was proved to have been wrong and St Paul right. But, consider the situation: the most junior of the apostles, a man who had never followed our Lord during his sojourn on earth, withstanding St Peter to the face with impunity! Could such a thing have been possible if there had been any idea at all in the Church that our Lord had granted universal jurisdiction to St Peter?

There is not one single text in the New Testament (and be it remembered that, except for one not vitally important "Epistle of St Clement", every bit of evidence for what the Church believed in the first century is contained therein) which even suggests that St Peter claimed any authority over the other apostles, or that anybody thought that his jurisdiction differed in any way from theirs. There is, however, one sentence which suggests that an apostle did claim some sort of authority of a universal nature. One of them wrote that he was weighed down by "the care of *all* the Churches".[2] That does suggest a claim to universal jurisdiction, and it is not difficult to imagine what Roman controversialists would have made of it if it had occurred in one of St Peter's epistles. But it does not. It was St Paul who used the expression. No one has ever suggested that St Paul claimed to be a Bishop of Bishops. The fact that he can use the phrase quite casually to indicate the abundance of his labours (nothing more), whereas if St Peter had used it in the same way it would have been twisted into a claim to universal jurisdiction, affords a good illustration of the way in which every possible reference to St Peter has been misinterpreted and exaggerated in order to justify the papal claims.

There may be an indication that some at least, realized the weakness of the case for the universal jurisdiction of the Pope, based on the current mistranslations and misapplications of Scripture, in the fact that attempts were made to support it by forgeries. Some time during the sixth century there appeared a document containing a fabulous account of Constantine's conversion and baptism, which was drawn up in a way which suggested that he

[1] Gal. 2.11.   [2] 2 Cor. 11.28.

had written it himself.[1] In it the Emperor ordered that all ecclesiastics everywhere should be subject to the Pope and he transferred to them "the city of Rome, and all the provinces, districts and cities of Italy and the Western regions". This, if it had been genuine, would have meant that Constantine divested himself of his authority at least over all Western ecclesiastics and transferred to the Pope the "overlordship" of the whole of the Western empire, at least so far as the Church was concerned. That Constantine's successors could possibly have been bound morally or legally by such an abdication is, at the very least, a matter of considerable doubt. But the question does not arise, because the document is universally recognized to be a forgery. It is not the only one.

About the middle of the ninth century there were published documents which came to be known as the Pseudo-Isidorian Decretals.[2] They were decisions of Popes and councils, part genuine, part forgeries, from the first to the eighth centuries. In them the Popes are made to claim for themselves universal jurisdiction. They limited the powers of archbishops by giving to all bishops a *right* of appeal to the Pope from their local provinces, and declared the freedom of all ecclesiastics from secular control.

The Papacy itself had nothing to do with the actual forgeries. They were not made at the direction of any Pope or, indeed, of any Church authority. But the age in which they appeared was an uncritical one, and they passed into Canon Law through Gratian's *Decretum*. The champions of the Church in the quarrels against secular sovereigns made great use of them to help their cause. They seemed to prove that right was on the side of the ecclesiastics who claimed immunity from the laws of their country. The forgeries were exposed in the fifteenth century, and to-day no Roman Catholic scholar would defend them, or base any argument upon them. But, as we have learned to our cost in the international sphere, a lie, if it gets a sufficient lead, creates an atmosphere which persists even after it is exposed. The rightfulness of the papal claims to jurisdiction, and to the independence of the "clergy" from secular control, were built up by falsehood, and

[1] Bettenson, *Documents of the Christian Church*.
[2] Cf. Kidd, *Documents*, III.

retained some glamour of divine right and legality, even after powerful instruments by which the impressions had been created had been proved to be unworthy. Even so to-day the belief of a divine grant of authority to St Peter, based upon a mistranslation of St Matthew, still persists although the errors are clear for everyone to see.

The Revival of the Empire

It was impossible to justify the universal jurisdiction of the Papacy, either out of the Scriptures, or by the tradition of the early Church. Nevertheless in a world in which all ordered government had ceased it became a fact. The Church, ruled by its hierarchy, was a unity, spread throughout all Europe. Thus when England was still divided into seven hostile kingdoms there was one Church of England, its bishops bound together by one ideal, administering their dioceses under the supervision of the arch-bishops, enforcing the laws, rules, and customs of the Church of the West. What was true of England was true of all Western Europe. The Church was a united body and, for reasons which we have considered, the Pope was its head. Presently, by the genius of Charlemagne, the warring tribes were welded into something like the old Empire, and the Frankish chieftain ruled effectively over an area almost as large as had ever been subject to the Western Emperors. In 800 Pope Leo III acknowledged the fact by crown-ing him. Through all the years of chaos men had looked back with longing to the old Roman peace, and Leo's act was welcomed everywhere, except, it seems, by Charlemagne himself. He knew that he was *de facto* Emperor and that no ceremony could add to his actual authority. It is very probable that Leo was in fact claiming in some way to be the superior of the Emperor; to be the Vicar of Christ, conferring a subordinate sovereignty, which, if it should be used wrongly he could take away. But, most certainly Charlemagne never saw himself as an agent of Leo. He was the Viceregent of God. It was God who had given him his sovereignty, and all that Leo had done was to recognize that fact and convey to him the blessing of the Church, that he might be aided to serve God faithfully in the office to which he had called him. It is significant that Charlemagne adopted the semi-ecclesiastical robes of the Eastern emperors. After his coronation he treated the Pope, not as another sovereign, still less as an overlord, but as the chief prelate of his realm. He himself ruled the Church, as well as the State, with a very firm hand. Although he allowed freedom of election to the Papacy, he appointed to other bishoprics throughout his dominions. He initiated missionary work on the fringes of his diocese. He wrote letters to abbots and monks lecturing them on their duties. He inspired a revision of the missal and breviary, and attempted to establish some uniformity in worship throughout his great empire. He introduced the custom of singing the creed at Mass into his private chapel, and it was from there that it spread throughout the West, although it was not adopted at Rome until 1014, after strong pressure had been brought to bear on the Pope by the Emperor Henry II. Charlemagne interfered in the iconoclastic controversy, supporting the heretical cause, and he was instrumental in the adoption by the whole Western Church of the *filioque* clause of the Nicene Creed. About all these matters he consulted bishops and theologians, but he acted on his own authority, and without any special reference to the Papacy. Everything that Charlemagne did proves that he was inspired by the old conception of the Emperor, the Priest-King, responsible to God and to God alone, for his rule, not only of the State, but of the Church as well.

Although some of Charlemagne's chief assistants were Englishmen, England itself never formed part of the Holy Roman Empire. Its Kings were always independent, even in theory. It is possible that they deliberately asserted this when they followed Charlemagne's example and adopted the ancient imperial robes. Our sovereigns are still anointed and crowned, wearing the semiecclesiastical vestments of the Eastern emperors. Although, like Charlemagne, they worked for the most part in harmony with their own ecclesiastics, like him they made and enforced laws for the Church, which they ruled as effectively as they did the State. It is beyond argument that they accepted the universal Western doctrine of the supremacy of the Popes in spiritual matters, but it is equally certain that they thought of their own sovereignty as received directly from God. When Pope Gregory VII demanded

10

that William the Conqueror, who had won his crown partly
through papal support, should do homage for his kingdom,
William refused "because neither have I promised it, nor do I
find that my predecessors did it to your predecessors".[1] A contemporary writer, a monk of Canterbury, tells us that William
would not allow anyone settled in his dominions to acknowledge
a Pope, save at his bidding, nor to receive letters from one until
the matter had first been approved by himself. He refused to allow
the archbishop, even in council with all the other bishops of the
realm, to frame any canons without his consent, and he insisted
that there should be no excommunication of any of his subjects,
even for the most heinous sin, "save by his command".[2] William
lived and died in full communion with the Papacy.

Consideration of the facts of the rule of a Justinian, a Theodosius, a Charlemagne, and a William I will show clearly what was in
the minds of the English reformers when they said in Article
XXXVII: "The King's Majesty hath the chief power in this
Realm of England, and other his dominions, unto whom the chief
government of all Estates of this Realm, whether they be Ecclesiastical or Civil, in all causes doth appertain . . . we give not to our
Princes the ministering either of God's Word, or of the Sacraments . . . but that only prerogative, which we see to have been
given always to all godly Princes in holy Scriptures by God himself." There was very considerable historical precedent for that
position and, as we have seen, not all "godly Princes" would have
wholly concurred in the limitation. Some most certainly ministered
"God's Word" in that they issued definitions of faith and enforced
right conduct, and did so with ecclesiastical approval.

The Developed Papal Claim

Papal authority grew up in the vacuum created by the abdication
of civil government. Its foundations were laid in the idea that the
priest is the prophet of God, declaring the law, which the lay
sovereign is bound to administer. Because the will of God is
declared through the priest he is, in that measure, the superior of
the King. The idea clashed directly with the older belief that the

[1] Kidd, *Documents*, III.   [2] Kidd, ibid.

lay ruler was God's viceregent, and the Middle Ages were filled with the struggle for supremacy between Church and State. A few illustrations of the position as seen through clerical eyes will make the anti-imperial theory clear. This is Gregory VII (1081) enunciating the faith as he sees it. "Shall not an authority founded by laymen . . . be subject to that authority which the providence of God Almighty has, for his own honour, established and given to the world?"[1] Gregory's Bull deposing the Emperor Henry IV contained these clauses: "To me has been given by God the power of binding and loosing in heaven and on earth. Relying on this . . . in the Name of God Almighty . . . I withdraw the whole kingdom from Henry . . . I absolve all Christians from the bond of the oath [of obedience and loyalty] made to him and I forbid anyone to serve him as king."[2]

In 1198 Pope Innocent III wrote

the Creator of the universe set up two great luminaries in the firmament of heaven; the greater light to rule the day, the lesser light to rule the night. In the same way . . . He appointed two great dignities; the greater to bear rule over souls (these being, as it were, days), the lesser to bear rule over bodies (these being, as it were, nights). These dignities are the pontifical authority and the royal power. Furthermore the moon derives her light from the sun, in both size and quality, in position as well as effect. In the same way the royal power derives its dignity from the pontifical authority.[3]

Here we have a clear expression of the thought that was probably in Pope Leo's mind when he "conferred the crown" on Charlemagne.

But even this does not mark the full extension of the papal claims. Boniface VIII in a Bull in 1302 said

there is one Church . . . one Head (not two like a monster), that is Peter, and the Vicar of Christ, who is Peter's successor. . . . In this Church there are two swords, viz. the spiritual and the temporal. . . . Both are in the power of the Church. But the latter is to be used on behalf of the Church, the former by the Church, the latter by the hand of kings and princes, but at the bidding of the priest . . . for the temporal power ought to be subject to the spiritual power. . . . Therefore we declare,

[1] Bettenson, *Documents of the Christian Church.*
[2] Bettenson, ibid.   [3] Bettenson, ibid.

state, define and pronounce that for every creature to be subject to the Roman pope is altogether necessary for salvation.[1]

As early as 1159 Alexander III had summed up the claim like this, "no one has the right to judge me, since I am the supreme judge of all the world".[2] We find that claim in action in Paul III's condemnation of Henry VIII (1535), although this Bull was never promulgated, for the Pope could not find any sovereign willing to execute his sentence. "We declare that Henry hath incurred the penalty of deprivation ... and if he depart this life we decree and declare, with the authority and fullness of power aforesaid, that he ought to be deprived of church burial and we smite him with the sword of anathema, malediction and eternal damnation."[3] The King's descendants, officials and subjects were all involved in the same sentence, unless they withdrew their allegiance from him.[4]

("For every creature to be subject to the Roman Pope is altogether necessary for salvation." But what happens when there is more than one Pope? Between the years 1000 and 1180 there were no less than fourteen anti-popes. What Petrarch called the "Babylonish Captivity" lasted for more than seventy years, during which period there were Popes living in Avignon as well as in Rome. The "Great Schism" was ended at the Council of Constance in 1415, when three claimants to the Papacy were deposed. The confusion and scandal created by the spectacle of two old men, each claiming to exercise supreme divine authority, and each cursing the other, was immeasurable. A contemporary of one of the schisms remarks that "for a long time Christians had had an earthly god who forgave their sins, but now they have two, and if one will not forgive them they go to the other". If really it is "necessary to salvation" to be subject to the Roman Pope, what happens to those unfortunate persons who in all good faith give their allegiance to a false one? Even now the Catholic Encyclopaedia is not quite certain about the claims of some Popes.)

The struggle between the two ideologies continued throughout

---

[1] Bettenson, ibid.
[2] See also Nicholas I (865) in Bettenson, ibid.
[3] Bettenson, ibid.
[4] For the Bull of Pius V excommunicating Elizabeth see p. 191.

the Middle Ages, with victories first for one side then for the other. In the end the Popes won their struggle against the empire. Some of the late medieval Emperors admitted that they bore rule "by the grace of God and the Pope". But, in truth, it was not the Popes who destroyed the empire, but the rising force of nationalism. It became impossible for one man to hold together so many peoples, who were beginning to think of themselves not as pledged to allegiance to some individual, but as Frenchmen, Bavarians, Austrians, Swiss, Spaniards, Venetians, bound together by a common tie of blood and language in loyalty to their land. No sooner had the Emperors established order in one corner of their vast dominions than a rebellion broke out in another. Gradually the various units secured their independence and "Emperor" became a title of honour without substance, The Popes abated none of their pretensions, but Kings, ruling firmly over compact nations, presented them with a problem very different from that of the old ramshackle empire. In our English histories much of the struggle goes by the queer name of the "Investiture controversy". The real principles for which both sides fought may be summarized in this way: "Bishops are very important to the State both because of political influence and financial power. Who appoints them? Are clerics exempt from the King's authority?" During this struggle St Anselm was banished and St Thomas à Becket was murdered. The battle seemed to have been won by the Pope when King John signed Magna Charta, for its first clause, "The Church of England shall be free", meant "free from royal control, and subject only to the Papacy". The position was determined in each generation, so far as England was concerned, not by the moral rights of the case, but by the personal character of the sovereign. When there were weak Kings the Church won freedom from royal control. When there were strong Kings there was always a determined attempt to make all clerics subject to the civil courts, to appoint as bishops men who were favourable to the royal cause, and force Churchmen to submit to taxation for royal purposes. The answers to the claims of the Papacy to overlordship were given by such Kings as William the Conqueror, Henry II, and Edward III. They are to be found in such enactments as the Constitutions of Clarendon (1164), and the Statutes of Provisors

(1351) and Praemunire (1353). "The Pope of Rome hath no jurisdiction in this realm of England."[1] This means that Henry VIII
not only repudiated every kind of interference in the affairs of the
Church of England, but he challenged also the doctrinal foundation by which all claims to rule and teach the Church had been
justified. Was he right or wrong in this? Was he right in claiming
that as God's viceregent he was supreme in his dominions—Head
even of the Church? That is the vital question at issue between
the Church of England and the Church of Rome.

Reasons for the Success of Henry VIII

Henry II and Edward III had tried to substitute royal for papal
political authority—and failed. They failed because the prestige
and popularity of the Popes was higher than theirs. But when
Henry VIII ordered his subjects to swear that they accepted him
as supreme Head of the Church, all save a tiny minority, in the
words of St Thomas More "signed merrily". "Merrily" may
seem a strange word to describe so violent a breach with tradition
in such a conservative country as England. How was it that the
authority of the Pope was renounced so easily, even in the spiritual
sphere, where it had always been accepted in England? The
reasons are many. First, the Bible having been translated, the
scriptural justification of the papal jurisdiction was seen to be
without foundation. Secondly, the Renaissance was bringing to
England the study of Greek and history and these had revealed
the ancient claims and practices of the Emperors. Thirdly, England
had come to maturity as a nation. The feelings of passionate
love and devotion for England, to which Shakespeare was
soon to give expression, were already filling men's hearts
and they welcomed any assertion of the independence of their
country.

But, probably more important than any other cause, there was
the character and conduct of the Popes themselves. Apply the
test "by their fruits ye shall know them" and few men have ever
looked less like the Vicars of Christ than did the Popes of the later
Middle Ages. The direct cause of the breach, as all the world

[1] Article XXXVII.

knows, was the Pope's refusal to grant a decree of nullity in connection with Henry's first marriage. This is often represented as a courageous stand by the Pope for moral principles. It was nothing of the sort. There is proof of this in the character of the prelates whom the Pope appointed to try the "King's matter". One, Cardinal Wolsey, was an Englishman and the other, Cardinal Campeggio, an Italian. Wolsey had a son, who was a priest, and a daughter, who was a nun, while Campeggio brought his son with him to England, and arranged for him to be knighted at the first tournament held after their landing. Ecclesiastics whose violation of the seventh commandment was so obvious can hardly have been appointed as judges of morals. In the eyes of the Pope the question was simply one of political expediency, camouflaged as legal principle.

There were many precedents for the decree for which Henry asked. For example, with the express approval of St Bernard, the marriage of Louis VI of France with Eleanor of Aquitaine had been dissolved on the same canonical grounds, although the marriage had endured for thirteen years and there were two daughters. Within a year Eleanor had married our own King, Henry II, without any ecclesiastical censure. The reason why Henry VIII did not get the freedom he desired had nothing to do with morals. Catherine of Aragon, his wife, was the aunt of the Emperor, who at that time had the Pope at his mercy. Here we touch upon the real reason why Englishmen had ceased to love and respect the Papacy: the degradation which had befallen the institution itself and the character and aims of the men who wore the triple crown. The Popes of the period were anything but Shepherds of the Flock of Christ. They were great secular potentates, greedy for power and wealth, Italian sovereigns, at war almost continuously with other princes. The stories of the Christological controversies make sad reading, but they are not so repulsively unchristian as those of the battles and sieges, treaties, alliances, intrigues, and breaches of plighted word which mark the struggle of the medieval Popes for a kingdom of this world. One Pope, John XXII, was elected in 1410 because he was a successful *condottiere*, a leader of mercenary soldiers. Professor Lodge says of him that "He seemed to be the only man who could be trusted to resist the threatening power of the King of Naples. But he had no pretensions to piety, or even respectability."[1] The Papacy became a great worldly prize, attracting careerists, who often secured their election by bribes. They lived in the greatest luxury and were concerned for the most part, not with devotion and the care of the Church, but with pleasure and the aggrandisement of their families. The money which they spent so lavishly on dissipation and the furtherance of their personal ambitions was bled from the faithful. Thus, every new appointment to an English benefice involved a "ransom" of one year's revenue. Bishoprics and abbeys were kept vacant so that the income accruing to them could be confiscated. Others were sold to the highest bidders, who were often Italians, or other foreigners, who drew their salaries from England, although they did no work in return, and indeed never left their own countries. The laity were subject to the tax known as Peter's Pence, although the "clergy" largely escaped national taxation. When lawsuits were carried to Rome it was necessary to pay heavy fees and bribes in order to get a case heard at all. Papal exactions steadily drained away the wealth of the nation. To what end? In order that the Popes might finance their petty wars, that they might build and decorate great churches and palaces and in order that they might live in more ostentatious luxury than any secular prince. Henry VIII grew to manhood whilst the Borgian Pope, Alexander VI, was reigning. Alexander's predecessor had been the first Pope to acknowledge openly his illegitimate children. Alexander certainly had ten such children and Bishop Creighton says of him that "the exceptional infamy that attaches to him is largely due to the fact that he did not add hypocrisy to his other vices"[2] as did most of the other Popes of that age. The later Middle Ages was a time of shocking immorality, but men claiming to be the Vicars of Christ, declaring that it was altogether necessary to salvation to be in communion with them, might have been expected to exhibit a higher standard of conduct than the other dissolute princes who surrounded them. Is it surprising that the people of England came to regard their pretensions to exercise the authority of our Lord as spurious?

[1] Lodge, *The Close of the Middle Ages.*
[2] Creighton, *History of the Papacy.*

With all his faults Henry VIII was a more respectable Head of the Church than these papal celibates. These things are horrible to write, and to read, but they must be taken into account if justice is to be done.

The adage that power tends to corrupt and absolute power corrupts absolutely has been illustrated in the story of both Church and Empire. The Emperors who strove for pre-eminence, and the Kings who attained it, were seldom examples of Christian life. But, after all, their kingdoms were of this world. The great tragedy of Christendom is that the men who claimed to be the Chief Shepherds of the Flock of Christ should have spent their lives also striving for temporal dominion, and riches. It is always a danger to think about any institution in the light of its appearance at the moment. But the Papacy, which to-day asks for no more sovereignty than is sufficient to ensure independence in spiritual matters, is almost a different institution to that which declared "by me kings reign and princes minister justice", which levied war, and taxed the world that it might make its standard of living the most luxurious in the world. If the isolation of the Church of England is to be understood and fairly judged it must be considered not in relation to the reformed Papacy of to-day, but against the background of the corruptions which made possible the repudiation of papal supremacy.

Conclusion

In the above pages an attempt has been made to set the conflict between the royal and the papal supremacy fairly in the context in which it was fought. Much can be said on both sides. It is not the kind of question in which all the right is on one side and all the wrong on the other. It is not possible to consider it without mixed feelings and perhaps most people, who try to understand it, will find that their attitude to it differs from time to time. The circumstances of to-day make it almost inevitable that this should be the case. When we resent, as we sometimes do, the harm done to religion by the many frustrations caused by the legal fetters which result from the State connection, our sympathies incline against the Crown. But, in fairness, we must remember that in the Middle Ages the Church of England suffered even more seriously from a diametrically opposite evil. When we applaud the glorious stand for liberty of conscience and worship made by Roman Catholics behind the Iron Curtain, we are tempted to think that their cause is the same as that of the medieval Church. But it is not. We are attaining, even if we have not fully reached, at least in England, an entirely new conception of the relation of the State to religion. This is that religion is not an affair of the State at all. Every citizen, who keeps the laws of his country, which should be concerned with earthly, not spiritual, affairs, ought to be free to believe and worship as he thinks right. But this solution of the problem was not even a dream in the sixteenth century.

We know that a divided Christendom is a scandal, for it is clearly contrary to the expressed will of Christ. As our bishops have repeatedly said at Lambeth conferences, it is not possible to conceive of a united Church without the Pope. We might all agree that in the Papacy the Holy Spirit has raised up an institution which, working as it does to-day, divorced from temporal power, may be not only of the greatest possible good, but one which is almost essential if unity is to be restored. For the moment papal policy forbids any such justifications of the Pope's supremacy and demands that the Papacy be accepted, not as a useful instrument of divine power in the present world, but as a divine institution from the beginning. This claim is at variance with both Scripture and history. Until it is modified we have no alternative. We must reject it and go on as we are.

But does that mean that we go on as Protestants who are cut off from the Catholic Church? Roman Catholics tell us that is the case. But is it? Although we may be tempted sometimes to view more leniently than our fathers the papal claims to jurisdiction, expressed as they must be in the less political and more spiritual terms of to-day, we have no right to forget the real points—which are these. Bearing in mind the extravagant claims of the Popes and their unworthiness in the past, the futility of the argument for them which was produced from the Scriptures, can it be maintained, with any show of reason, that by repudiating the papal jurisdiction the Church of England did something so manifestly contrary to the will of our Lord, that it ceased to be the Catholic Church in our country? Bearing in mind the facts of the rule of what our Articles call "godly princes", can it be maintained, with any show of reason, that by preferring royal to papal supremacy the Church of England cut itself off from the unity of Christ's Church? In view of the fact that the Eastern Churches are undoubtedly orthodox, and that even Rome admits the validity of their sacraments, can we possibly believe that "to be subject to the Roman Pope is altogether necessary to salvation"? It is to that outrageous belief that those who submit to Rome must subscribe.[1] It is submitted that the throwing off of a yoke, unknown in primitive times, consistently repudiated by the East, fashioned by misapplications of Scripture, supported by forgery, which moreover had been so abused that it had become unbearable, could not possibly have unchurched the Church of England.

[1] See Appendix F.

CHAPTER 17

"THE CHURCH OF INNOVATIONS"

UP TO the point where we began to consider the Papacy, the argument was that the Prayer Book proves that the Church of England is not a new institution, founded at the Reformation, but that it is the continuing Catholic Church in our country. To call it, as its enemies have done, and still do, the "New Religion" is to contradict the facts. Now it is necessary to take the offensive and to consider how far Rome can claim to be the "Old Religion". To any English Catholic this must be an exceedingly distasteful work, even when it is remembered that Rome never ceases to attack the Church of England. Roman controversialists ridicule its claim to be the ancient *Ecclesia Anglicana*. They deny the validity of its Orders and sacraments and do all in their power to entice its children from their Mother Church. Nevertheless, although the necessities of defence, which is a filial duty, involve some attack, it is possible to do so only at the price of a very heavy heart. For if Canterbury is our mother, Rome is our grandmother, and to-day at all events, English Catholics have no desire at all to judge her. They do not believe that the Pope is a "bishop of bishops", but if non-Anglican bishops choose to allow him the jurisdiction which that title claims, they do not consider it any business of theirs. Our Anglican bishops do not accept the papal claim to be by divine appointment the Vicar of Christ, in the sense that it is through the Pope that all grace flows to the episcopate, the priesthood, and the faithful, and they regret that the Popes should make such a claim.[1] But no English Catholic doubts that the Pope's place in the Church is of exceeding great importance and that he has a primacy of honour.

Part of the defence of the Church of England against Roman attack lies in the assertion that in some respects Rome is a New

[1] Cf. Appendix F. It was formally made by St Thomas Aquinas. Cf. Medley, *Church Universal.*

Religion. Although, of course, it has continued in essentials the ancient Catholic teaching and practice of the Church, nevertheless in doctrine it has been responsible for several startling novelties. If a Protestant be defined as one who protests against the Catholic Church, then the Easterns are justified in asserting that Rome is the "Mother of Protestants", for Rome has promulgated doctrines which are manifestly new. The Easterns, in an official letter to Pope Leo XIII,[1] made the following assertions: "The present Roman Church is the Church of Innovations, of the falsification of the writings of the Church Fathers, and of the misinterpretation of the Holy Scripture and of the decrees of the Holy Councils." "Falsification of the writings of the Church Fathers" occurred in the Forged Decretals. "Misinterpretation of the Scriptures" is the basis of the papal claims to supremacy and infallibility. For "misinterpretations of the decrees of the Holy Councils" one illustration must suffice. Pope Zosimus in 419 claimed *on the authority of the Canons of Nicea* that bishops who had been disciplined by their province had a right to appeal to Rome. The African bishops found that their copies of the canons contained no such provision, so they wrote to the great patriarchates for information. It was proved that the Council of Nicea had not sanctioned such a right of appeal and the Council of Carthage, in 424, reporting this fact to Rome, used language which amounted to a strong censure for the Pope's false claim.

Perhaps it will be best to quote the whole paragraph in which the Easterns accuse Rome of innovations.

For the holy purpose of union, the Eastern Orthodox and Catholic Church of Christ is ready heartily to accept all that both the Eastern and Western Church unanimously professed before the ninth century,[2] if she has perchance perverted, or does not hold it. And if the Westerns prove from the teaching of the Holy Fathers and the divinely assembled Oecumenical Councils that the then Orthodox Roman Church ever before the ninth century read the Creed with the addition that the Holy Ghost proceeded from the Father "and the Son", or used unleavened bread, or accepted the doctrines of a purgatorial fire, or sprinkling

[1] To be found in full in Lowndes, *Vindication of Anglican Orders*, Vol. II.

[2] The significance of the "ninth century" is that the Easterns are prepared to accept all that the Church taught before the Great Schism.

instead of baptism, or the Immaculate Conception of the ever-Virgin, or the temporal power, or the infallibility and absolutism of the Bishop of Rome, we have no more to say.

To these accusations of innovation are added in other places in the encyclical four more—the teaching that at Mass consecration is effected, not through the invocation of the Holy Ghost, but "along with the utterance of the Lord's words—Take eat" etc.; the withdrawal of the chalice from the laity; the Treasury of Merits; the teaching that the saints already enjoy the Beatific Vision.

When the Easterns say that all these things were unknown before the ninth century, when the Church was still visibly one, they are speaking the truth. But a novelty is not necessarily false. In some of these accusations the Church of England is implicated, for they are an inheritance from the Middle Ages. The use of the *filioque* clause in the creed, the use of unleavened bread, teaching about the moment of consecration, the "pouring" (not "sprinkling" as the Easterns state) of water at baptism, as a permitted alternative to immersion, are all matters which the Church of England continued. We no longer come into condemnation for witholding the chalice from the laity. Nor are we implicated in Roman errors connected with the Treasury of Merits, or the condition of the souls of the departed. Some facts about all these points will be found elsewhere in this book. But there are two very important matters to be considered now: the innovations concerned with the infallibility of the Pope and the Immaculate Conception of our Lady. To these Anglicans must add the Assumption of our Lady.

The Infallibility of the Pope

Papal "infallibility" does not mean papal "impeccability", although some non-Romans think that it does. No Roman Catholic believes that the Pope cannot sin. It is just as hard for a Pope to live a good life as it is for any other Christian. All that infallibility means is that when as Vicar of Christ, and successor of St Peter, the Pope makes a solemn pronouncement about faith or morals the Holy Spirit will preserve him from error. This is the decree of infallibility, issued by Pius IX in 1870.

We [this is the royal plural] adhering faithfully to the tradition received from the beginning of the Christian faith—with a view to the glory of our Saviour, the exaltation of the Christian religion, and the safety of the Christian peoples (the Sacred Council approving) teach and define as a dogma divinely revealed: that the Roman Pontiff, when he speaks *ex cathedra* (that is, when—fulfilling the office of Pastor and Teacher of all Christians—on his supreme apostolical authority, he defines a doctrine concerning faith or morals to be held by the Universal Church) through the divine assistance promised to him in blessed Peter, is endowed with that infallibility which the Divine Redeemer has willed that His Church—in defining doctrine concerning faith or morals—should be equipped: and therefore that such definitions of the Roman Pontiff of themselves—and not by virtue of the consent of the Church—are irreformable. If anyone shall presume (which God forbid) to contradict this our definition; let him be anathema.[1]

The Eastern bishops state their case against infallibility in these words:

The Orthodox Eastern and Catholic Church of Christ, with the exception of the Son and Word of God, knows no one that was infallible on earth. Even the apostle Peter himself, whose successor the pope thinks himself to be, thrice denied the Lord and was twice rebuked by the apostle Paul, as not walking uprightly according to the truth of the gospel. Afterwards Pope Liberius in the fourth century subscribed an Arian creed; and likewise Zosimus, in the fifth century, approved an heretical confession, denying original sin. Vigilius in the sixth century was condemned for wrong opinions by the Fifth Oecumenical Council and Honorius, having fallen into the Monothelite heresy, was condemned in the seventh century as a heretic, and the popes who succeeded him accepted his condemnation.

The Easterns are right in all their facts. These will now be considered in turn, beginning with St Peter, although in order to make the argument sound this necessitates going again over some of the ground of the last chapter. There will be, however, a slight difference in the presentation. There we considered the papal claim to sovereignty; now the point at issue is the claim to be the divinely appointed and inspired Teacher of the Church. If the promise in Matthew 16, on which the claim to infallibility is usually based, meant what Rome now declares it meant, our Lord must have made St Peter at that time the foundation Rock of the Church, and presumably endowed him with infallibility. Unfortunately the very next recorded incident proves that St Peter

[1] Bettenson, *Documents*.

remained an exceedingly fallible man, and that about a matter of
faith. For the next recorded incident is this: "From that time
forth began Jesus to show unto his disciples how that he must go
up to Jerusalem, and suffer many things . . . and be killed. . . .
Then Peter took him, and began to rebuke him, saying, Be it
far from thee, Lord: This shall not be unto thee. But he turned,
and said unto Peter, Get thee behind me, Satan: thou art an offence
unto me: for thou savourest not the things that be of God, but those
that be of men."[1] To be called Satan and told that he was a
stumbling-block would have been a very curious beginning to an
infallible career. But, as is shown in Chapter 16 above, our Lord
made no grant of authority of any kind to St Peter at that time.
It is a Roman misinterpretation to change a promise "I will
build", "I will give" into an immediate action and gift. There is
nothing in the New Testament to indicate that anybody ever
thought of St Peter as infallible, and a great deal which suggests
exactly the opposite. There is, for example, the situation referred
to by the Easterns. St Peter had been granted the vision[2] of "the
sheet let down from heaven" in order to teach him that since the
Atonement cleansing of mankind there has been "nothing common
or unclean". He interpreted his vision as meaning that Gentiles
were to be admitted freely to the Church. But afterwards he
"separated himself [from Gentiles] fearing them that were of the
circumcision".[3] St Paul says that about this matter he "resisted him
to the face, because he stood condemned".[4] In this very important
matter infallible Peter was proved wrong, and a junior apostle,
who said of himself that he was "the least of the apostles" and
"not worthy to be called an apostle"[5] was proved right. All this
happened after Pentecost. The matter was one which affected the
very life of the Church. Its solution in St Peter's way would have
meant that Christianity would never have become a world-wide
Catholic Church, but would have remained an obscure sect of the
Jews. If the man upon whom the whole theory of infallibility is
based could have been fallible about so fundamental a question,
how can his successors have inherited infallibility from him?
    The facts about Pope Liberius are these. When Constantius, a

[1] Matt. 16.21.   [2] Acts 10.   [3] Gal. 2.12.
[4] Gal. 2.11. (R.V.)   [5] 1 Cor. 15.9.

convinced Arian, became sole ruler of the empire in 353, he banished St Athanasius and terrorized most of the bishops of the Church into adopting an Arian creed. At Councils held at Arles (353) and at Milan (355) the Western bishops abandoned Athanasius and entered into communion with Eastern ones who had previously subscribed to the heresy. But Pope Liberius stood firm for orthodoxy. In consequence he was banished and an Arian anti-pope was enthroned in Rome. Unhappily Liberius grew weary of exile. He made peace with the Emperor and was allowed to return to Rome and fight it out with his rival. The price he paid was the abandonment of St Athanasius and the signing of an Arian creed. Dr Leighton Pullan states that evidence, which is almost contemporary, "makes it extremely probable that he signed what was known as the Blasphemy"—the most extreme expression of the heresy. But whether Liberius accepted this, or some semi-Arian formula, "he signed as *de jure* Bishop of Rome, who wished once more to be Bishop of Rome *de facto*. Whatever he signed, he abandoned St Athanasius and lapsed into heresy."[1]

About 409, an Irish monk, called Pelagius, began to teach a new heresy. He asserted that as Adam was created perfect, so is every man sinless at birth. The handicap of original sin is an illusion. By his own will and effort every man can win salvation. Pelagianism minimizes sin and does away with the need for a saviour. It paves the way for a denial of the Atonement, and more remotely of the Incarnation also. It leads to a repudiation of the sacraments. In 416 the African bishops condemned the heresy and excommunicated Caelestius, its ablest teacher. Pope Innocent I concurred in the sentence. In 417 he was succeeded by Zosimus, who re-examined the teaching of Caelestius and Pelagius and declared them orthodox. He wrote blaming the African bishops for their action and he received the heretics into communion. The Africans replied by repeating their condemnation. At this point the Emperor entered into the controversy on the orthodox side, and banished Pelagius. Zosimus at once "saw the light" and joined in the condemnation of the heresy. There is no doubt, however, that the Pope, either through incompetence, or wilfulness, for a

[1] Pullan, *The Church of the Fathers.*

11

time condoned a deadly heresy, and supported men whom the united Church has anathematized.

The case of Pope Vigilius is not so clear. It is very hard indeed to find the path through the interminable Christological controversies, which were sadly complicated by political aims, and which were fought out with appalling bitterness during the fifth and sixth centuries. The Empire of the West had been overrun and broken up by the barbarians, and the first faint shadows of dissolution were falling upon that of the East. Egypt was on the point of asserting its independence. Religious controversy was hastening the decay. The Emperor Justinian, in an attempt to placate the Egyptians, issued an edict condemning a summary of the teaching of certain religious leaders, whom the Egyptians detested, but which under the title, "The Three Chapters", had been approved by the General Council of Chalcedon (451). The edict was badly received, and the Latin bishops rejected it outright. Justinian then summoned Pope Vigilius to Constantinople, where he gave "a pitiable example of irresolution. He accepted, rejected, censured and was complaisant in turns."[1] At last he agreed to the summoning of a General Council. It met in 553 at Constantinople and is known as Constantinople II. At the last moment Vigilius withdrew and refused to have anything to do with it. Nevertheless it supported the Emperor in the condemnation of the Three Chapters which the West had refused to endorse. Vigilius would not sign and was sent into exile. But after six months he accepted the decrees, and was allowed to return to Rome. He found that Milan and North Italy had broken off communion with him. The schism lasted for more than fifty years. It seems probable that Vigilius was never a formal heretic, but his indecisions contributed to the bitterness which separated Egypt from the Orthodox Church and this renders him particularly obnoxious to the Eastern bishops. He did reject for a time the decisions of what was eventually recognized as the Fifth General Council. He was followed in 557 by Pope Pelagius (not to be confused with the heretic of the same name). Pelagius could find only two bishops willing to consecrate him and he "won acceptance by the Romans only by rejecting a formal statement of his predecessor".[2]

[1] Hutton, *The Church and the Barbarians*.   [2] Ibid.

The Mohammedan menace to the Eastern Empire led in the seventh century to an attempt to end the Egyptian schism. The Patriarch of Alexandria, encouraged by the Emperor Heraclius, suggested to Pope Honorius a formula of belief, which he thought was orthodox. The Pope thought so too, and accepted it. Later it was seen that this new Egyptian statement was as dangerous to the Catholic faith in the true humanity of our Lord as the one which had caused the schism. It was condemned by the Sixth General Council (Constantinople III) in 681. Although Honorius had died, this council anathematized him by name and Pope Agatho, who had succeeded him, was instrumental in securing the condemnation of his predecessor. To us, to-day, the controversies associated with the fifth and sixth General Councils seem to be somewhat empty disputes about words. But, as a matter of fact, any doctrine which minimizes either the real divinity of our Lord, or alternatively his true manhood, undermines that faith in the Incarnation which is fundamental to the Christian religion. When therefore we find that some Popes took the heretical side in any of these controversies and were afterwards condemned by Councils which both East and West acknowledge to be true General Councils, and that their successors approved the condemnations, we are faced with a fact of major importance. It clearly contradicts the declaration of Leo X (1513) that "it is clear as the noonday sun that the Popes, my predecessors, have never erred in their canons or constitutions".[1] Indeed, he was contradicted by a Pope, for a Bull of Paul IV (1555) says "when it is discovered that a Pope has at any time been heretically or schismatically minded all his subsequent acts are null and void",[2] a statement which would have been meaningless if Leo X had been right. In spite of Leo, there is no doubt at all that Liberius lapsed into Arianism and Zosimus into Pelagianism and that anathemas pronounced upon Vigilius and Honorius by universally acknowledged General Councils were confirmed by their successors.

If these are the facts, how can the doctrine of papal infallibility be maintained? Only on the assumption that when Popes fell into error they were not speaking *ex cathedra.*

Turn back to the Decree. There is scarcely a sentence in it

[1] Quoted by Quirinus.   [2] Bull, *Cum ex apostolatus officio.*

which does not suggest an untrue idea. It is unnecessary to deal again with the assumption that the Pope is the "supreme Pontiff, the Pastor and Teacher of all Christians", or that our Lord promised any special assistance to St Peter. But three new points call for special notice:

1. That it is only *ex cathedra* pronouncements which are infallible.
2. That to contradict an *ex cathedra* pronouncement involves anathema.
3. That infallibility resides in the Pope himself, and not "in the consent of the Church".

The first point immediately raises the question, "What constitutes an *ex cathedra* statement?" The curious answer is that "nobody knows". The conditions which lift a decision above ordinary ones, and invest it with infallibility, have never been declared. For example, was the decree of the Immaculate Conception of our Lady (1854) an infallible one? Was the recent decree of her Assumption infallible? Nobody knows. To contradict them involves excommunication and to disbelieve them secretly is declared to be a mortal sin. Yet, however unlikely it may seem to-day, it is not utterly impossible that they could be "reformed" at some future date, as was the decree of Eugenius IV, supported by the Council of Florence (1438), which declared that the "Matter" of Holy Orders was the delivery of the "Instruments". As we have seen[1] this decree was reformed by the present Pope in 1948. But how can the faithful distinguish between Eugenius and Pius? Why is Pius right and Eugenius wrong? Pius says "it is not lawful for any man to infringe this our Constitution secretly, nor boldly to oppose it". Is his therefore an infallible decree? Both the dogmas of the Immaculate Conception and the Assumption were issued with great solemnity and it has been declared necessary to salvation to hold them, for to deny them involves being cut off from the Body of Christ. Nevertheless some Roman Catholics doubt whether they are infallible decrees. The fact is that unless, and until, the conditions which mark an infallible

[1] Chap. 8.

decree are defined, no decision of any Pope can be recognized certainly as such.

But although it is not possible to say what makes a decision, in the words of Pius IX, "irreformable", nevertheless the Roman Church has a way of marking some decrees as especially important. Ordinary decrees of the Inquisition, the body which is concerned with orthodoxy, are issued on any day of the week, except Feria V, which is Thursday. On that day the Pope presides over its deliberations, so that decrees issued on Thursday have the additional prestige of his formal approval. They are intended to be irrevocable and final. But on Feria V, 25 February 1616, and again on Feria V, 15 March 1616, Pope Paul V issued a decree declaring "that the earth moves daily is absurd, philosophically false, and theologically considered at least erroneous in faith". This was repeated by Pope Urban VIII on Feria V, 30 June 1630. Be it noted that this is said to be a matter of faith. Three times it was repeated on the day of the week reserved for decisions pronounced with the utmost solemnity. But was it an *ex cathedra* statement? Since no one to-day would attempt to maintain that it was true, Romans would say that it was not. But they can hardly deny that it was intended to be taken very seriously. Again, the decree of 1948 was clearly intended to be final—so final that the Pope said that no one must infringe it, even "secretly". It is mortal sin to think in one's heart that the Pope has made a mistake about it. But was this an infallible pronouncement? Nobody knows. We may well ask, "What is the true value of papal infallibility, when it is completely impossible, even for Roman Catholics, to ascertain when it has been exercised?"

The answer is that the definition of papal infallibility was a political, rather than a religious, move. The key is to be found in the dogma itself. The *ex cathedra* definitions of the Roman Pontiff are said to be "irreformable of themselves", and not by virtue of the consent of the Church. Behind this statement there is a long history of conflict.

When the Popes were left the only representatives of central authority in the West, the Papacy gradually became a prize, desired by ambitious men. Therefore it was inevitable that the papal throne, like any other, should become a source of struggle, struggle between Roman factions, noble Italian families, and national powers, and equally inevitable that from time to time evil men should win it. Some of the pontiffs were so intolerably evil that they had to be deposed. Sometimes groups of cardinals declared the throne vacant and elected a successor. At times the Emperors interfered. The usual appeal was to a General Council.

But if there was any one thing of which the Popes were certain, it was that they were the Vicars of Christ, and therefore the highest authority on earth. The case was put very clearly by Paul IV (1555). "The Pope judges all, but is judged of no man."[1] Although it is often suggested that this doctrine is based upon the New Testament, as a matter of fact it originated in a slowly developed custom of appeals to the Popes, which was founded upon the ancient appeals to Caesar, and buttressed by such documents as the Forged Decretals, and the forged Donation of Constantine.[2] The Decretals state that "the Church of Rome, by a singular privilege, has the right of opening and shutting the gates of heaven to whom she will". In the Donation, Constantine is made to say, "inasmuch as our imperial power is earthly, we have decreed that it shall venerate and honour the most holy Roman Church and that the sacred see of blessed Peter shall be gloriously exalted above our Empire and earthly throne". The position is quite logical if the premises are true; if in Rome, to quote the Donation again, "the rule of priests and the Head of the Christian religion have been established by the Emperor of Heaven".

It was natural that the worst Popes, those whom it was most necessary to depose, should cling determinedly to the doctrine of their divine right. When Councils had been called to deal with the scandals of their rule, they moved heaven and earth to prevent any infringement of their prerogatives. Although some of them were deposed, on the whole they were successful in their aim. So long as the Petrine texts in the gospels were interpreted wrongly, and before such documents as the Forged Decretals had been exposed, it was well nigh impossible to resist the conclusion that, although the actual wearer of the triple crown might be unworthy of his office, that office was of divine appointment. But, if this was indeed the case, then it must be true that the Pope who judges all men is judged by none. Every interference, whether by

---

[1] Bettenson, *Documents*.   [2] Bull, *Cum ex apostolatus officio*.

ecclesiastical or secular authority, tended to weaken that position. The Papacy brushed aside the claims of civil rulers by asserting the superior right of the "spirituality" and its claim to speak in the name of God. But to secure it from the threat of ecclesiastical Councils something more was necessary. This "something more" was found in the Infallibility Decree.

The struggle between the Papacy and the upholders of the Conciliar theory continued throughout the late Middle Ages. Ultimately the Popes were victorious, but not until the Reformation had torn half Western Europe out of the unity of the Church. The shock of that loss had two great results—the moral abuses connected with the Papacy were corrected, and in the Society of Jesus the Popes found an army wholly devoted to their cause. The Jesuits believed that, in order to win back the lost ground, it was necessary for Catholics to present the Protestant enemy with an absolutely united front. To achieve this, so they thought, all ecclesiastical authority had to be centralized in Rome and the Pope had to be set high above all criticism. They fought, therefore, to extinguish local liberties and to substitute papal nomination for canonical election of bishops. An episcopate nominated by the Pope could be trusted to be loyal to him. Both of these aims are manifest in the struggle against Gallicanism, and in those which brought about the downfall of the great abbey of Port Royal and all but wiped out the ancient Church of Holland. The means by which in the two latter cases the Jesuits achieved their ends were wholly discreditable. They produced a number of propositions, which everyone agreed were heretical, and persuaded the Pope to condemn them as included in a book about St Augustine, which had been written by Jansen, Bishop of Ypres. Both the nuns of Port Royal and the Catholics of Holland were willing to denounce the heretical statements, but they were unable to consent to the proposition that they were contained in a book, in which certainly they were not. This was declared to be heresy. The Pope's word must be accepted, even in a matter of fact.[1] Wholesale

[1] A semi-official explanation of what this means is to be found in the *Clergy Review* for October 1950. Canon G. D. Smith states that the Pope by defining a doctrine makes it part of the "Deposit of Faith", even if it was unknown to the Church until the fifth century.

excommunications followed. Port Royal was suppressed. The Dutch dioceses were pronounced incapable of electing their bishops and their Church was put under the jurisdiction of vicars-general appointed directly by the Pope.[1] The Old Catholic Church of Holland is the surviving remnant of the Catholics who would not submit to this treatment. Neither the primitive nor the medieval Church was totalitarian, as the almost unending struggle against the claims and demands of the Popes abundantly proves. It was the Jesuits who contrived to concentrate all ecclesiastical power in the hands of the Popes. Through their work that became the fact in all parts of the Church which remained within the Roman communion. The theory by which the papal autocracy was finally justified was that of infallibility.

The Jesuits showed their hand as early as 1611. They proposed to establish, in a public disputation before Louis XIII, three propositions:

1. The Pope is infallible in judging faith and morals.
2. In no case whatsoever is a Council superior to a Pope.
3. It belongs to the Pope to determine doubtful questions, and to confirm or disallow the decisions of Councils.

The disputation never took place, because the University of Paris vetoed the public discussion of propositions which were clearly heretical in that they contradicted the decisions of the Council of Constance (1414). But the goal had been declared, and the Jesuits and their Ultramontane allies worked unceasingly until it was reached in 1870.

The decree of infallibility brought to an end, so far as Roman Catholics are concerned, both the long struggle between the Papacy and secular governments and that between the Papacy and the Conciliar theory. The Pope may still take counsel with the bishops, if he cares to do so, but now they are not so much bishops of the Church as his bishops. Decision rests with him alone, and when once he has declared anything, all Roman Catholics must accept what he says, without reservation and without further discussion. The faithful may not even doubt "secretly" the truth of what he says.

[1] For the full story of this see C. B. Moss, *The Old Catholic Movement*.

The fact that there is no certainty about the conditions which constitute a declaration an *ex cathedra* one is not a disadvantage from the papal point of view. On the contrary, it makes the position watertight, for as a result of this uncertainty any papal pronouncement *may* be infallible. To harbour doubts, still more to deny openly anything at all, which the Pope declares, however trivial, *may* be to oppose the Holy Spirit. It *may* be mortal sin. It *may* render the offender liable to damnation. For it is laid down in the decree itself, that to contradict an infallible pronouncement involves anathema. Since it is always uncertain what sayings of the Pope are infallible he must always get his own way, for the dangers of disagreeing with what may possibly be an infallible utterance are too great to risk. Thus the whole edifice of papal power is secure. No appeal to history, or Scripture, or universal tradition, or reason, or common sense, has any validity. The Pope speaks and the case is finished, for God has spoken through his Vicar. The pronouncement may destroy regulations in force since the days of the apostles, as the recent dispensation from the eucharistic fast did. It may contradict flagrantly those of earlier Popes—as we have seen has happened again and again. These things do not matter. It is rebellion to point out inconsistencies. It is the utterance of the moment which matters. Any earlier pronouncements, with which it is not in harmony, must be explained away somehow or other. The latest teaching stands, and must be defended. It is simply not possible to imagine a position more remote from that laid down by St Vincent of Lerins in the fifth century and accepted as Catholic by the universal Church ever since. The Catholic, he says, will fortify his faith "in a two-fold manner, firstly by the authority of God's law, then by the tradition of the Catholic Church".[1] Tradition is necessary, because Scripture is so profound that "all men do not place identical interpretations upon it".[2] Therefore "in the Catholic Church we take the greatest care to hold that which has been believed everywhere, always and by all".[3] It will be noted that the infallibility decree directly contradicts St Vincent, for the decree by-passes both Scripture and tradition, to rest in a personal infallibility, so that "*ex cathedra* definitions of the Roman Pontiff of

[1] Giles, *Documents*.   [2] Ibid.   [3] Ibid.

themselves—and not by virtue of the consent of the Church—are irreformable".

This is a new thing. In the beginning, for all his force of character and power of leadership, St Peter was one apostle amongst many. In the same way his successors were bishops amongst equals, although a vague prerogative of honour was allowed them from very early times. It was the sort of primacy which the Archbishop of Canterbury holds in the Anglican communion. It developed as time went on, and there was no great harm in that. Our Lord expressly said that the Holy Spirit would guide the Church into all truth. It may well have been his intention that there should be a visible centre of unity, and, so to speak, a permanent president of the episcopate. We can see that it might be a very great service to the Church that there should be such an institution as the Papacy. But that Peter should dictate to Caesar, and even on occasion attempt to depose him; that he should teach without contradiction Paul, and James, John and Andrew—that is a very different matter. That is a very new idea in the Church. There is no doubt at all that the Easterns are right when, in this matter, they accuse the Roman Church of innovation.

The facts cited above are facts. Most of the foundation ones can be verified simply by consulting a New Testament. The others can be checked by anyone who has access to a reasonably good library. They prove that infallibility is worse than a myth. It is a blasphemous deceit. It is based on falsehood. It is false to say that our Lord made St Peter the foundation rock of the Church. It is false to say that our Lord promised to St Peter, or to his successors, any especial divine assistance. It is false to say that our Lord equipped either St Peter, or the Popes, with infallibility. It is false to say that St Peter himself was infallible, or that the Popes, his successors, have been infallible. On the contrary the truth is that St Peter erred about a matter of faith, even after the Pentecostal outpouring of the Holy Ghost, and Popes have erred time and again, and contradicted one another with monotonous frequency.

The Immaculate Conception of our Lady

In 1854 Pope Pius IX defined the dogma of the Immaculate Conception, and made it a necessary article of belief for Roman Catholics. The definition runs:

We, with the authority of our Lord Jesus Christ, the blessed apostles Peter and Paul, and with our own, do declare, pronounce and define, that the doctrine which holds that the Virgin Mary was, in the first instant of her conception, preserved untouched by any taint of original guilt, by a singular grace and privilege of Almighty God, in consideration of the merits of Christ Jesus the Saviour of mankind—that this doctrine was revealed by God and therefore is to be firmly and steadfastly believed by all the faithful. Wherefore if any shall presume (which God forbid) to think in their hearts anything contrary to this definition of ours, let them realize and know well that they are condemned by their own judgement, have suffered shipwreck concerning the faith, and have revolted from the unity of the Church. . . .[1]

It is important to realize exactly what this definition means, for many oppose it, even bitterly, for things which it does not say. This is to be regretted, for some of the things which it does say are sufficiently evil. The points to notice, as officially explained, are seven:

1. Our Lady was preserved from original sin by an act of God, not by her own merits or effort.
2. This took place at the "first instant of her conception", which was completely normal. The parents of Mary are in no way concerned with her immaculateness. That took place at the moment, whenever that is, when God creates and infuses a rational soul into the animal body.
3. Adam and Eve were created sinless. By their fall they injured the human nature, which they transmitted to their offspring. Because God willed that in his Son mankind should be given a fresh start, he willed that the second Adam should be born with the same sinless nature with which Adam was created. Therefore his mother, the second Eve, was preserved from the inheritance of original guilt in order that she might not transmit the infection to her Son.

[1] Bettenson, *Documents*.

4. This was done by virtue of the anticipated merits of Jesus Christ, the Saviour of all mankind, including his mother. Mary owed her holiness to the grace of her Son, and both her immaculate conception and her subsequent freedom from actual sin were by virtue of the fore-known merits of the atonement later made on Calvary.

5. Two objections, therefore, which Protestants often allege against the doctrine are simply non-existent. It does not contradict the doctrine of the unique sinlessness of our Lord. He was tempted like all men, but conquered by virtue of his own merits. Mary was preserved from original sin by the application of his merits, and she conquered actual sin through his prevenient grace. Secondly, the doctrine asserts no more than that, because of his love for us, God caused the Mother of the Saviour to start her life with the same advantage that he gives to every Christian at baptism—no more, no less.

6. The doctrine is stated to be of divine revelation.

7. It is declared to be "necessary to salvation".

It is clear that if the whole of this body of doctrine can be regarded as speculation, there is very little, if any, harm in it. Except for the last two, none of the points contradict in any way the established faith of the Church. If they were advanced as pious opinions anyone might hold them without blame. "There has never been any real question in the Church of the sinlessness of Mary from her birth, although a few Fathers before the Council of Ephesus do charge her with venial sins. But it is no less true that some also use language about our Lord, which could not have been used after the definitions made at the great Councils."[1] The Easterns hold firmly the belief that our Lady was free from actual sin, although they repudiate the dogma of her Immaculate Conception. Thus Professor Lossky writes, "she was holy and pure from her mother's womb, but not with a sanctity which places her outside of the rest of humanity-before-Christ. She was not in a state analagous to that of Eve before the fall at the moment of the annunciation . . . she was without sin under the universal

[1] Bede Frost, *The Mystery of Mary.*

sovereignty of sin, pure from every seduction in a humanity enslaved by the prince of this world."[1] Between this Eastern and Western view there is little more than a disagreement about the moment at which our Lady reached absolute sinlessness. Both agree that she was free from actual sin and that this was due to the grace of God, but whereas the Romans believe that in order to fit her for her peculiar vocation this grace was given to her, by a singular privilege, at the moment when she began to be a human being, the Easterns, it appears, would teach that she had to wait for the outpouring of the Precious Blood on Calvary before the inherited taint of human nature was washed away. The difference would have mattered very little, if it had not been for the two points now to be considered.

Pius IX declared that the doctrine, which he defined, had been divinely revealed. But when? To whom? Not to the apostles, for there is not the very slightest hint of it in the New Testament. Not to the Fathers, for there is no trace of it in their writings. The great Councils of the Church never mentioned it. Clearly it has not the authority of the undivided Church, for the Easterns have always repudiated it, and great Western theologians have denied it. It first became an object of interest and controversy in the tenth century, and most of the Doctors of the Western Church were opposed to it. St Anselm taught that our Lady was conceived and born in sin. St Bernard believed that she was conceived in sin, but sanctified before birth. St Thomas Aquinas agreed with St Bernard. So, surprisingly, for he was a Franciscan, did St Bonaventura. As a general rule the Dominicans followed St Thomas Aquinas in opposing it. The Franciscans, led by Duns Scotus, were the chief upholders of the doctrine. Although the Dominicans were the great scholars, the Franciscans had the more popular appeal and slowly their opinion prevailed. Pope Pius IX could say truly that he was declaring a doctrine which, by his time, the vast majority of Roman Catholics had come to hold, although even then controversy had not quite ceased and there were distinguished theologians who rejected it. The only basis for the Pope's statement that the doctrine was divinely revealed is his own authority as Pope. What that is worth we have seen when papal infallibility

[1] V. Lossky, *The Mother of God.*

was considered. Is there any doubt at all that the Eastern accusation of innovation is justified?

It was bad enough that the Pope should proclaim a doctrine for which there was no Catholic authority. It was far worse that he should anathematize those who in their hearts find it impossible to agree with him. To say that those who are unable to accept his innovation and who think secretly in their hearts that his definition is untrue, are "self condemned, have suffered shipwreck concerning the faith, and have cut themselves off from the Church", is utterly monstrous.

The Assumption of our Lady

The Easterns do not accuse Rome of innovation because of the definition of the dogma of the Assumption. It is probable that the doctrine was first believed in the East, but the East holds it with a difference. For the East considers that it is an error to believe that there is "a full reward for the just before the universal resurrection and judgement".[1] In this matter there is some inconsistency. For although the Easterns affirm the Assumption, which suggests that our Lady has already entered into her glory, nevertheless on occasion they pray for her, a thing no Westerner would dream of doing. Anglicans must accuse both East and West of innovation in this matter—if the doctrine be taught as part of the Deposit of Faith and therefore "necessary to salvation". What is the doctrine? It is that after her death the soul of our Lady returned to her body and her entire person was lifted up to heaven, so that she lives now complete, body and soul, in glory. In her case God has anticipated that which, St Paul tells us, is his will for all members of Christ on the day of resurrection. "The dead shall be raised incorruptible, and we shall be changed. For this corruptible must put on incorruption, and this mortal must put on immortality. But when this corruptible shall have put on incorruption, and this mortal shall have put on immortality, then shall come to pass the saying that is written, Death is swallowed up in victory."[2] The Dogma of the Assumption declares that in the case of our Lady the day of resurrection has already come. We shall see that there

[1] Orthodox Encyclical.   [2] 1 Cor. 15.52–4.

are reasons for believing that this doctrine, which is held by the East as well as by Rome, may indeed be true, and we may be glad that the Church of England nowhere condemns it, so that as a pious opinion any Anglican is free to hold it, without censure. Our quarrel, if we have one, is with both the East and Rome, not because they believe it, nor even because they keep a festival in commemoration of it, but because of the importance which they attribute to it. Rome now teaches that the doctrine must be held on pain of anathema, and it seems as if the East also teaches that it is part of the deposit of faith, and, in consequence, that it is binding on all loyal members of the Church.

But the Assumption of our Lady cannot be part of "the faith once delivered to the Saints".[1] There is not one particle of evidence to show that it was known before the fifth century. Every clause in the Universal Creed can be supported by clear scriptural texts. Not so the Assumption. St Paul, who tells us so much about the resurrection body, and about the ascension of our Lord, preserves complete silence about our Lady. If he had believed in the Assumption it would have been very natural, when telling us that "flesh and blood cannot inherit eternal life"[2] until it has been changed, to have added "as we know the body of the second Eve has already been changed". But he does not. In the whole of the New Testament there is not one single reference to our Lady's old age or death, still less to her Assumption, and the embarrassment which this has caused liturgically can easily be seen by studying the "proper" for her feasts. The oft-quoted text in the Apocalypse about the "woman clothed with the sun"[3] is not easy to interpret. Probably it is a reference to the Church. Certainly it does not refer to our Lady in glory. The context makes that absolutely certain. We have to wait until the fourth century for any mention at all of our Lady's death and when it comes it tells against a belief in an assumption. St Epiphanius, about 375, wrote, "I do not say that she remained immortal; but neither do I assert that she died." It would seem that St Epiphanius thought it possible that our Lady escaped death, like Elijah, and like him was taken up alive into heaven. He suggests this, but he says that he does not know. It is clear that when he wrote there could have been no

[1] Jude 3.   [2] 1 Cor. 15.50.   [3] Rev. 12.1.

tradition of an assumption in the circles in which he moved. Indeed we have to wait another hundred years for the first story of the death and resurrection of our Lady. Then it appears amongst writings which pretend to be the work of such people as St Bartholomew, St Joseph of Arimathea, and St Thomas, but which the Church has denounced as impudent forgeries.[1] They bear the same relation to the canonical scriptures as many of the popular pseudo-historical novels of to-day do to the teaching of the Church. They vary from pious fiction to poisonous heresy. One of these, known as the *Transitus Mariae*, pretends to have been written by St John the Evangelist, although it is a heretical work of the fifth century. From this a writer called the pseudo-Dionysius, because he pretends that he is Dionysius the Areopagite, the Athenian convert of St Paul, constructed a story upon which St John Damascene drew. It is this last account from which the Roman Breviary lessons for the day are taken. This is not a tradition of which any Christian can be proud!

Some illustrations of these fables may help towards an understanding of the position. This is one of the earliest. It was written, or pretends to have been written, by Theodosius, Patriarch of Alexandria. "At the tenth hour there were thunderings and a choir of angels was heard and David's harp. Jesus came on the chariots of the cherubims, with the soul of the Virgin seated in His bosom, and greeted us [SS. Peter and John]. He called over the coffin, which had been shut like Noah's Ark, and it opened. The body arose and embraced its soul, even as two brothers, and they were united the one to the other." Another account, said to be that of St Joseph of Arimathea, tells how the apostles were transported on clouds suddenly from the ends of the earth to Jerusalem, where our Lady was lying ill. Christ came down with a host of angels and took the soul of his mother. "The earth shook, and all Jerusalem saw the death of Mary in one instant." The body was buried. But Thomas did not arrive for the funeral. He came just in time to see the holy body being taken up to heaven, and our Lady threw down to him her girdle. When he met the other apostles he denied that her body was in the tomb and Peter rebuked him, reminding him of his doubts about the resurrection

[1] Collected by James, *The Apocryphal New Testament*.

of our Lord. Because he insisted that the tomb was empty, it was opened and found to be as St Thomas had said. Then Thomas showed the girdle and all rejoiced and "the same clouds which had brought them now carried them back". This story is "dated" by the fact that St Thomas relates that he was caught up while saying Mass and before he could change his "priestly vestments". It was not until the sixth century that certain old-fashioned clothes began to be considered "priestly". In some of the stories the apostles, and others, are said to accompany our Lady to Paradise, and even, in one, on a visit to the nether regions also. So these stories go on, fantastic detail being added to fantastic detail, contradiction following contradiction. What is probably the earliest account is attributed to Evodius (usually described as the first bishop of Antioch, but here Archbishop of Rome), the successor and spiritual son of St Peter, who insists that he was an eyewitness of all he relates! The Assumption is said to have been witnessed by no one, by St Peter and St John, by all the apostles, by St Thomas alone, by many of the faithful of Jerusalem. It is said to have taken place on the day of our Lady's death, and on the third, the eighth, the sixteenth and the two hundred and sixth day after her burial. Is this really an event, belief in which is necessary for salvation?

It is not at all likely that faith in the Assumption originated in these fantastic stories. In all probability their invention was to popularize something which was already widely believed. In any case the credulity of heretics outside the Church does not prove that, as a matter of fact, our Lady's body was not taken up into heaven. We know that the festival of the Assumption was the earliest festival of our Lady to be observed and that both East and West began to celebrate it without any controversy arising about it.

Why was this? Surely because although there is no historical evidence for the fact, there are theological reasons which make it exceedingly probable. God's character, as Holy Scripture reveals it to us, makes it very likely that he would have exalted the Mother of his only Son to the highest heaven. There are three arguments in particular which point to that conclusion. 1. In the Scriptures death, in the sense of the corruption of the body, is always regarded as the consequence and punishment of sin. "By envy of

12

the devil came death into the world."[1] "Death [came] by sin."[2]
But the Church has never doubted that our Lady was sinless.
Belief in the justice of God demands that she, who was free from
the cause of corruption, should escape its punishment. 2. Scripture
presents our Lord to us as perfect God made perfect man. Perfect
man means that in all his relations with his mother he was
without flaw. He took his perfect human nature from Mary—he
was bone of her bone, flesh of her flesh. When his work on earth
was finished that human nature was exalted into heaven. If he
allowed the body of his mother, from which he had received that
which was now glorified, to rot in the tomb, could we really talk
about the perfection of his human nature? Would that have been
the act of a perfect *human* son? 3. Our Lord promised special
favours to those who had continued with him in his temptations.[3]
No one was with him so intimately as the mother who bore him in
her womb, cared for him in childhood, and stood beside his cross.
He promised that the gift even of a cup of cold water should be
rewarded. Mary nourished him at her breast. Shall she be un-
rewarded? Surely justice demands that her utter faithfulness
entitles her to a special reward, which can never be taken from
her. But what does justice suggest that her reward should be?
Mary was with the Lord in the closest possible way in the time of
his humiliation, therefore it is fitting that she should be wholly
with him in his glory. All this means that she must be in heaven
in the same way in which her Son is there, that she must be with
her Son in the body from which he took his own. To deny such
deductions as these would be to build up a case for the imperfec-
tion of our Lord. There are very many who react from this so
violently that they celebrate the Assumption with joy and thank-
fulness, because they feel that it safeguards the faithfulness of God
and the perfect holiness of their Saviour.

But if that is so, why should Anglicans be concerned about the
promulgation of the dogma of the Assumption? Because the
definition has, as it were, added a new clause to the creed. To say,
as the united Church did say, that the arguments in favour of the
Assumption are so strong that it is permissible to celebrate it with

[1] Wisd. 2.24.   [2] Rom. 5.12.
[3] Luke 22.28.

a festival of "Devotion" is one thing. It is a wholly different matter to assert that belief in it is necessary to salvation.

In face of the evidence it is not possible to maintain that the infallibility of the Pope, or the Immaculate Conception, or the Assumption were ever part of the original "deposit of faith".[1] They are not definitions of doctrine which has always been part of the Church's treasury of truth. They are new dogmas which have been added to the "Faith once delivered to the Saints". To assert that the faithful must believe them—not merely not deny them openly, but must believe them in their hearts—on pain of damnation, is a monstrous abuse of authority. The Easterns are justified when they assert that "the present Roman Church is the Church of innovations". The Church of England, which Roman Catholics accuse of having broken away from the ancient faith and practice of the Church, has never done anything half so serious. Are not Anglicans justified if they remind them of the old proverb "those who live in glass houses should not throw stones"?

[1] See note on page 155.

CHAPTER 18

THE NEW RELIGIONS

BEFORE trying to see the whole picture, the details of which we have been considering, it will be as well to attempt some comparison of the doctrines and practices of the Church of England with those of the Protestant connections who gloried in the fact that they had broken away from the medieval Church. This will give us a chance to ask the question, "Is there any justification for placing the Church of England amongst the religious bodies which are truly representative of the New Religions?" In fairness, it must be remembered that they all believe that they have restored the "set-up" of the Apostolic Church. We are not considering, now, whether there is any truth in that claim. We are simply asking the question, "Is the Church of England one of the bodies which broke, in the Protestant fashion, with the Church of the Middle Ages?"

In order to compare in some detail the doctrines of the New Religions with those of the Church of England, for the Church of England we will go to the Prayer Book and Articles. The Protestant position will be illustrated by quotations from their authorized statements of faith and from Luther and Calvin, who for many separatists occupy the position which "Doctors" hold in the Catholic Church. We are confronted here with what is a constant difficulty in all our controversies. Not the Roman Catholics, nor the Protestants, nor we ourselves, have come unchanged through the centuries. We have all had to adapt ourselves to new habits of thought, so that we find ourselves attacking positions long abandoned. It is highly probable that to-day not many dissenters in England still hold these views. Some may even detest them as much as any Catholic. But it was because of such views that the Church was rent by schism in the sixteenth century and the question is, did the Church of England throw in its lot with the innovators? It is in order to make quite clear the crucial points that some words in the quotations are italicized.

God's Purpose in Creation

The New Religions	The Church of England
"All men are not created on an equal footing, but for some eternal life is preordained, for others eternal damnation." Calvin's *Institute* (1539)	"Predestination to Life is the everlasting purpose of God." Article XVI
"God hath, *before the foundation of the world*, foreordained some men to eternal life, to the praise and glory of His grace, leaving the rest in their sins, to their just condemnation, to the praise of His justice." Baptist: *First Confession* (1646)	"O Merciful God, who hast made all men and hatest nothing that thou hast made, nor wouldest the death of a sinner . . . Have mercy upon all Jews, Turks, Infidels and Heretics . . . that they may be saved." Collect for Good Friday
"Original sin is seen to be an hereditary depravity and corruption of our nature . . . *Whatever is in man*, from intellect to will, from the soul to the flesh, *is all defiled* and crammed with concupiscence." Calvin's *Institute*.	"Original sin . . . is the fault and corruption of the Nature of every man . . . whereby man is very far gone from original righteousness, and is of his own nature *inclined to evil*, so that the flesh lusteth always contrary to the spirit." Article IX
"Our first parents . . . became dead in sin and wholly defiled . . . the guilt of their sin was imputed, and the same death in sin and corrupted nature conveyed, to all their posterity . . . whereby *we are utterly indisposed and made opposite to all good* and *wholly inclined to evil*." Presbyterian: *Westminster Confession* (1643)	

Predestination and Election

These are extremely difficult subjects to epitomize shortly. Sometimes people who are not very familiar with St Paul's epistles and such writers as St Augustine, accuse the Church of England of having fallen into heresy in Article XVII. But there is no doubt at all that a form of predestination is taught in Holy

Scripture and that St Augustine gave the imprimatur of his great authority to some form of the doctrine. In Scripture, as in Catholic writers, predestination is always balanced by other statements, and in consequence has not the force of God's direction of men's lives towards salvation or damnation, but rather of his foreknowledge of the way in which each individual will respond to the grace which is freely offered to all. In Catholic theology stress is laid on our Lord's words "many are called but few are chosen".[1] Many are called, because, it would be taught, all are called. "Never would God have created anything, if he had hated it."[2] Our Lord cries, "Come unto me, *all* ye that labour and are heavy laden".[3] If few are chosen at the last, it is because few choose to accept that invitation. But "he that cometh to me, I will in no wise cast out"[4]—that is God's predestination. Man has free will. He is created for eternal life and is offered it. If he does not choose to accept it, the blame is his, not God's.

Turning to the specific teaching in Scripture about predestination, on the one hand we have St Paul's clear statements in the Epistle to the Romans. "Whom he did predestinate them he also called, and whom he called, them he also justified".[5] "Shall the thing formed say to him that formed it, Why hast thou made me thus? Has not the potter power over the clay, of the same lump to make one vessel unto honour, and another unto dishonour? What if God, willing to show his wrath, and to make his power known, endured with much long-suffering the vessels of wrath fitted to destruction: and that he might make known the riches of his glory on the vessels of mercy, which he had before prepared unto glory."[6] St Paul is here justifying the action of God in rejecting the ancient chosen people and electing the Gentiles into their place. He long endured the wickedness of the people, whom he had created for blessing, but who chose to disobey him. When they have filled up the cup of their wickedness cannot God elect less blessed nations into their place? That is the gist of St Paul's arguments. He does not say that anyone at all was created for "dishonour", but only that God has power so to create, if he should so desire.

[1] Matt. 22.14. [2] Wisd. 2.24. [3] Matt. 11.25.
[4] John 6.37. [5] Rom. 8.30. [6] Rom. 9.20–3.

All this must be balanced by other passages in the Scriptures. For example, St Paul himself says "God, our Saviour, who will have all men to be saved and come to the knowledge of the truth".[1] Also, St John wrote "Jesus Christ the righteous: and he is the propitiation for our sins; and not for our sins only, but also for the whole world."[2] The fact of the matter appears to be that, just as in the doctrine of the Blessed Trinity we have to combine two apparently contradictory facts—that God is three Persons, although there is but one God—so here the Bible lays down apparently contradictory truths, both of which must be held by him who would hold the whole truth. God's universal love and desire for the salvation of every child, and his foreknowledge that some will choose to separate themselves from him, are both taught. So also is the difficult conception that although God knows who will choose life, freedom of choice has been given to all. Although we cannot see, at present, how these revealed truths are completely compatible with one another, yet, if in the interests of logical consistency, we are led to deny any one, we shall find ourselves involved in far greater difficulties. It is the Catholic balance of doctrine which the Church of England contrives to hold even in Article XVII.

"By predestination we mean the eternal decree of God, by which he has decided in his own mind what he wishes to happen in the case of each individual. For all men are not created on an equal footing, but *for some eternal life is preordained, for others eternal damnation.*"

Calvin's *Institute*

"Everlasting God, who, of thy tender love towards *mankind* hast sent thy Son, our Saviour . . . to suffer death upon the cross, that *all* mankind should follow . . ."

Collect for Palm Sunday

"God to carry out his judgements directs the councils and excites the wills (of those whom *he is rightly said to blind, to harden and to turn*) *through Satan*, the minister of his wrath."

Calvin's *Institute*

"Almighty . . . God . . . who hatest nothing that thou hast made, and dost forgive the sins of all them that are penitent . . . the God of all mercy."

Collect for Ash Wednesday

[1] 1 Tim. 2.3,4.

[2] 1 John 2.1.

"By the decree of God, for the manifestation of his glory, some men and angels are predestined unto everlasting life, and others foreordained to everlasting death ... Neither are any redeemed by Christ ... but the elect only. The rest of mankind God was *pleased* ... to pass by and *to ordain* them *to dishonour* and wrath."

Presbyterian :
Westminster Confession

"The moving or efficient cause of predestination to life is not the prevision of faith, or of perseverence, or of good works, or of anything which may be in the person predestinated, but only the will and the good pleasure of God. Of the predestinated there is a *forelimited and certain number*, which can neither be diminished nor increased."

The Lambeth Articles (1596)

"Jesus Christ by his death did purchase salvation for *the elect* that God gave unto him. *These only have interest in him* and fellowship ... The free gift of eternal life is given to them, and none else."

Baptist : *First Confession*

"Thou art the same Lord, whose property is *always* to have mercy."

Prayer of Humble Access

"O God, who declarest thy *almighty power* most chiefly in showing mercy and pity."

Collect for Trinity XI

"Almighty God, our heavenly Father, who of thy tender mercy didst give thine only Son Jesus Christ to suffer death upon the Cross ... who made there ... a full, perfect, and sufficient sacrifice, oblation, and satisfaction for the sins of the *whole* world."

The Communion Service

Final Perseverance

"They whom God hath accepted can neither totally nor finally fall away from the state of grace; but shall *certainly persevere* therein to the end and be eternally saved."

Presbyterian :
Westminster Confession

"Let us, while we have the light, believe in the light, and walk as children of the light; that we be not cast into utter darkness ... Let us not abuse the goodness of God."

Commination Service

"I heartily thank our heavenly Father that [by baptism] he hath called me to this state of salvation, through Jesus Christ our Saviour. And I *pray* unto God . . . *that I may continue* in the same."

Catechism

"Deliver us not into the bitter pains of eternal death . . . Suffer us not, at our last hour, for any pains of death, to fall from thee."

Burial Service

The Rule of Faith

For all the New Religions, except such sects as the Quakers, the only source of authority in the Church was the Bible, which was regarded as self-interpreting. The Church of England clung to the ancient doctrine that the Church is the divinely appointed Teacher of Truth. It preserved the creeds as the dogmatic expressions of essential belief, and for both faith and practice appealed to the tradition of the Church. Of this tradition the Bible was the most important strand, for it contains all that has survived of the belief and custom of the Church of the apostolic age—that is to say of the men who had known the Saviour during the days of his ministry. Therefore to the Bible the Church of England appeals so that it accepts nothing as essential to salvation which cannot be proved from it. In this it is but following the customs of the age of the great Councils. The Church of England does not desire, or attempt, to hamper legitimate development, but it refuses to acknowledge anything which the Bible does not contain as part of the Faith delivered to the saints by the apostles, and therefore part of the essential Deposit of Faith. But for the interpretation of Scripture it turns to the Church and especially to the creeds and the definitions of the acknowledged General Councils.

"The authority of the Holy Scripture . . . dependeth not on any man or Church; but wholly upon God . . . the author thereof . . .

"Holy Scripture containeth all things necessary to salvation : so that whatsoever is not read therein, nor may be proved thereby, is not

The infallible rule of interpretation of Scripture is the Scripture itself."

Presbyterian:
Westminster Confession

"The rule in which is contained the whole duty of man . . . is only the Word of God, contained in the Scriptures, which are the only rule of the holiness and obedience for all Saints, at all times, in all places to be observed."

Baptist: *First Confession*

"Revelations of God by the Spirit, whether by outward voices and appearances, dreams or inward manifestations in the heart, were of old the formal object of their faith and remain yet so to be." "From these revelations of the Spirit of God . . . have proceeded the Scriptures . . . nevertheless . . . they are not the fountain, therefore they are not to be esteemed the principal ground of all truth and knowledge, nor yet the adequate primary rule of faith and manners."

Quaker:
Fifteen Propositions (1678)

to be required of any man, that it should be believed as an article of the Faith, or be thought requisite or necessary to salvation."

Article VI

" *The three Creeds* . . . ought thoroughly to be . . . believed."

Article VIII

"The Church hath power to decree Rites and Ceremonies and authority in Controversies of Faith."

Article XX

"It is evident unto all men diligently reading holy Scripture and ancient Authors."

Preface to Ordinal

"Here you have an Order for Prayer, and for the reading of the holy Scripture, much agreeable to the mind and purpose of the old Fathers."

Preface, "Concerning the Service of the Church"

"Granting some Ceremonies convenient to be had, surely when the old may be well used, they cannot reasonably reprove the old only for their age, without betraying their own folly. . . . For . . . they ought rather to have reverence unto them for their antiquity . . . "

Preface, "Of Ceremonies"

The Church

There is a sense in which Catholics acknowledge that the Church is invisible, for they believe that only God can read the hearts of men and therefore only he can know those who love and serve him in sincerity. On the other hand all the Protestant reformers did not deny that there is a sense in which the Church is visible. Thus the *Westminster Confession* states "the catholic or universal

Church, which is invisible, consists of the whole number of the elect. The visible Church, which is also catholic, or universal under the Gospel, consists of all those throughout the world that profess the true religion together with their children." This conception falls far short of the Catholic one, which includes the saints and the faithful departed in the unity of the Body of Christ. The Protestants would seem to have little, if any, idea of the "Communion of Saints".

In addition to this lack, the gulf which was dug between Catholic and Protestant about this question was the result of placing the emphasis in a different way. As it had always been, for the Catholic it remained impossible to belong to the invisible Church apart from membership in the visible one, and the faithful use of the sacraments, by which that membership was ministered and continued. For the Protestant the all-important points were the arbitrary election of God and the emotional response of faith to his calling. Some refused to acknowledge even that this response must bear fruit in holiness. All considered that the visible Church and its sacraments had very little bearing on the ultimate salvation of the soul.

The Church of England has nothing to say about the Invisible Church, and this is rather surprising at a time when a vast amount of hypocritical nonsense was being talked about it. It teaches that the Visible Church may be distinguished by its adherence to the Faith and by a lawfully appointed ministry and valid sacraments, two of which it declares to be "necessary to salvation". Also, rather strangely, it uses no hard words about the Pope. It does not deny that he has a prerogative of honour and precedence. It contents itself with saying that he has no jurisdiction in the English "realm", and although at that period this included the English Church, yet by refraining from saying so, it does not build up a barrier against some future reunion. It is noteworthy that, when violent abuse was customary, neither the Prayer Book nor the Articles embodied any denunciation of the Roman Catholic system. "Romish" doctrines were not official teaching, but popular misconceptions and superstitions.

"The catholic or universal Church, which with respect to the internal   "The visible Church of Christ is a congregation of faithful men, in

work of the Spirit and truth of grace, may be called invisible, consists of all the whole number of the elect."

Baptist: *Second Confession*

the which the pure Word of God is preached, and the Sacraments be *duly* ministered."

Article XIX

The Pope

"There is no other head of the Church but the Lord Jesus Christ. Nor can the Pope of Rome be head thereof; but is that Antichrist, that man of sin and son of perdition that exalteth himself *in the Church* against Christ."

Baptist: *Second Confession*

"The Bishop of Rome hath no jurisdiction in this *Realm* of England."

Article XXXVII

Holy Orders

"Whatever has undergone baptism may boast that it has been consecrated priest, bishop and pope, although it does not beseem everyone to exercise these offices . . . No man may take it upon himself without the wish and command of *the community*. And if it should happen that a man were appointed to one of these offices and deposed for abuses, he would be just what he was before . . . Therefore a priest should be nothing in Christendom but a *functionary*: as long as he holds his office he has precedence; if he is deposed of it he would be just what he was before."

Luther's *Appeal* (1520)

(There is nothing in the Protestant connections which corresponds to the formal granting of authority by authority, which the Church of England continued.)

"*Almighty God* . . . who of thy divine providence *hast appointed* divers Orders in thy Church."

Ember Week Prayer

"It is not lawful for any man to take upon himself the office of public preaching, or ministering the Sacraments . . . before he be lawfully called and sent . . . those we ought to judge lawfully called and sent, which be chosen and called to this work by *men who have public authority given unto them . . . to call and send*."

Article XXIII

"How weighty an office and charge ye are called . . . to be messengers, watchmen, and stewards of the Lord."

Ordering of Priests

"Will you be faithful in Ordaining, sending, or laying hands upon others?"

Consecration of a Bishop

"No man shall be . . . suffered to execute any of the said functions [Bishop, Priest, and Deacon] except he . . . hath had . . . Episcopal Consecration or Ordination."

Preface to Ordinal

"Receive the Holy Ghost . . . Whose sins thou dost forgive they are forgiven . . . And be thou a faithful dispenser of the Word of God, and of his Holy Sacraments."

"Take thou authority to preach . . . to minister the holy Sacraments in the Congregation, where thou shalt be lawfully appointed thereunto."

Ordination of a Priest

The Sacraments

"A sacrament is a *testimony* of God's grace to us confirmed by an external sign with our answering witness of piety towards Him."

Calvin's *Institute*

"Sacraments are nothing else than outward signs of our profession and fellowship."

Hermann (1547)

Christ has instituted "two . . . sacraments which are generally [universally] *necessary* to salvation."

Catechism

A sacrament is "an outward and visible sign of an inward and spiritual grace, given unto us, ordained by Christ himself, as a *means* whereby we receive the same and *a pledge* to assure us thereof."

Catechism

"Sacraments [are] *effectual signs* of grace."

Article XXV

Baptism

"Grace and salvation are not so inseparably annexed to it [Baptism] that . . . all who are baptised are undoubtedly regenerated."

Westminster Confession

"Seeing . . . that this child *is* . . . *regenerate* and grafted into the body of Christ's Church."

Baptism Service

> "Baptism, wherein I *was made* a
> Member of Christ, the child of
> God, and an inheritor of the king-
> dom of heaven."
>
> Catechism

Confirmation

The adherents of the New Religions left confirmation out of
their systems as a sacramental means of grace. The Church of
England not only retained it but tightened up its discipline concerning it, making it obligatory before first communion.

> "Ye are to take care that this child
> [just baptized] be brought to the
> Bishop to be confirmed."
>
> Baptismal Service

> "And there shall none be admitted
> to the holy Communion until such
> time as he be confirmed, or ready
> and desirous to be confirmed."
>
> Order of Confirmation

Absolution

(There is nothing which corresponds with this in any of the
Protestant connections.)

> "Our Lord Jesus Christ, who hath
> left power to his Church to absolve
> all sinners who truly repent and
> believe in him, of his great mercy
> forgive thee thine offences: And
> by his authority committed to me,
> I absolve thee from all thy sins. In
> the name of the Father" etc.
>
> Visitation of the Sick

Holy Communion

Whereas the Church of England made provision for daily
celebrations of Holy Communion, its importance was minimized
by all the Protestant sects. None would have declared that it was
"necessary to salvation". For most of them the elements, even

when being received, were no more than symbols. Nowhere does the Church of England make use of such a term.

"If it is true that the visible sign is offered to us to attest the granting of the invisible reality, then on receiving the symbol of the body, we may be confident that the body itself is no less given to us."

Calvin's *Institute*

"The communion of the Body and Blood of Christ is inward and spiritual . . . of which the breaking of bread . . . was a figure . . . even as abstaining from things strangled and from blood . . . yet seeing they are but shadows of better things, they cease in such as have obtained the substance."

Quaker. *First Principles*

Communion is universally "necessary to salvation".

Catechism

"*The Body of our Lord* Jesus Christ, which was given for thee, preserve thy body and soul."

Words of Administration

"The Body and Blood of Christ which are verily and indeed taken and received by the faithful."

Catechism

"The Body of Christ is given taken and eaten."

Article XXVIII

"Grant us . . . so to eat the Flesh of thy dear Son Jesus Christ, and to drink his Blood, that our sinful bodies may be made clean by his Body, and our souls washed through his most precious Blood, that we may evermore dwell in him, and he in us."

Prayer of Humble Access

"Grant that we receiving these thy creatures of bread and wine . . . may be partakers of his most blessed Body and Blood."

Prayer of Consecration

Communion of the Sick

The Protestant reformers made hardly any provision for the administration of the Viaticum, or for any communion of the sick. From their point of view it was unnecessary, for if the sick were "elect" they were saved, whatever their life might have been. If they were not elect they were damned, and no absolution, or communion, could help them. The English Protestants protested violently against sacramental provision being made for the sick and dying, but they did not gain their point. The Church of England made careful preparation for the confession, absolution, and communion of the sick in the services for their visitation and communion.

The Eucharistic Sacrifice

"In this sacrament Christ is not offered to his Father, nor any real sacrifice made at all . . . but only a commemoration . . . so that the Popish sacrifice of the mass is most abominably injurious to Christ's only sacrifice."

Westminster Confession

The sacrament was ordained "for the continual remembrance of the sacrifice of the death of Christ".

Catechism

"Accept this our sacrifice of praise and thanksgiving." (Eucharist)

Prayer of Oblation

The new doctrines opened up a gulf between Catholic and Protestant which still yawns between them. There is no neutral ground between people who believe that God created *all* men with a purpose of love and "willeth that all men should be saved"[1] and those who believe that he created some for the purpose of condemning them to everlasting punishment. There is no accommodation possible between those who hold that salvation is by faith alone and those who hold that, since our Lord said they were, baptism and communion are necessary also. Those who think that the really important thing about the true Church is that it is composed of members whom God elects and who are known only to him are irreconcilably opposed to those who believe that it was founded by our Lord a visible body, with a ministry authorized and commissioned by him with an outward sign, which is given through a hierarchy which stretches back to his apostles. There is no agreement possible between people who believe that, once "elected" by God, final perseverance and salvation are assured, and those who understand the Scriptures to mean that it is always possible to fall from grace, and that since it is only by "diligence" that we can make our calling and election sure, Christians must therefore use all the sacraments, which God has given for their

[1] 1 Tim. 2.4.

aid, and strive by prayer and obedience to his law, with penitence, "to work out their own salvation with fear and trembling".[1] There is no common platform on which people, who hold that the Holy Spirit teaches the faithful through the Church, the Body of Christ, "the pillar and ground of truth",[2] the guardian of the Christian tradition, so that by his inspiration it is enabled to interpret the Scriptures, can meet those who are convinced that any Christian can discover the truth for himself. These positions are wholly irreconcilable. One is that of the New Religions and the other that of the old Faith. On which side of the fence that separates Catholic from Protestant is the Church of England to be found? Compare again the quotations from official sources— and judge. Is it not utterly ridiculous to say that the Church of England aligned itself with the New Religions?

[1] Phil. 2.12.   [2] 1 Tim. 3.15.

CHAPTER 19

A HOUSE DIVIDED

THERE is no doubt that it is quite fair for enemies of the Church of England to accuse it of being a house divided against itself and to remind us that our Lord told us that such a house cannot stand. It would be absurd to attempt to deny that when members of the Church of England come together "everyone hath a psalm, hath a doctrine, hath a tongue, hath a revelation, hath an interpretation".[1] There could hardly be greater confusion; we must allow that to our enemies. But however divided and erroneous the opinions of the individual members of the Church of England may be, the Church of England itself has one clear voice and that speaks in the Prayer Book. There and there alone is the authoritative Church of England and in it there is no compromise. Members, even officers of the Church, are sometimes heretics. They do and say things for which there is no defence possible. That is true. One reason is that the Church of England developed the legal idea of the "parson's freehold", and the law is always very zealous in preserving rights of property. Benefices, including sees, carry with them such rights. In consequence the State has obtained such a stranglehold on the Church that when people are unfaithful there is no alternative—save bringing a lawsuit in a secular court, which may cause grave scandal—to tolerating the evil. But what the Church can do in these circumstances it does. It states quite clearly its faith and practice. If the fact that it feels it impossible at present to enforce these at law "unchurches" it, then that position must be accepted. But does it? This is not the only period of history when the Church has been powerless to do more than declare the truth.

We, who live to-day, are not responsible for the "parties" in the Church of England. They are the result of its history. From the earliest days of the Reformation the Church has had to fight

---

[1] I Cor. 14.26.

against enemies whom political reasons entrenched in its system, and who have sought to destroy its Catholic character. It has also had to fight against those who wished to take away its liberty and bring it again under the yoke of a foreign jurisdiction. But these latter enemies, from mid-Elizabethan times, have not been the great danger. The real threat has come from the Protestant extremists. It is quite clear now that what Elizabeth and her chief advisers desired was to restore, after the disasters of Mary's reign, the position as it had existed at the death of Henry VIII—that is to say, complete Catholicism without the Pope. But Elizabeth's Parliaments were made up of men, newly enriched by the pillage of the monasteries, who were inspired by fanatics returned from exile on the Continent. Such men all wanted a "root and branch reformation". Only so would their plunder be quite safe. Because of the hostility of the great foreign Catholic powers, and the criminal activities of the papists at home, Elizabeth was forced to rely on her Parliaments. But neither she, nor her council, could be bullied into doing the parliamentary will in religious matters. The facts of the situation, as brought to light by the latest research, will be found admirably set forth in a recent book by Professor J. E. Neale, *Elizabeth I and her Parliaments*. These facts afford a clue to something which has puzzled many scholars and lawyers who have studied the Prayer Book. What is the reason for the exceedingly curious wording of the Ornaments Rubric, which was incorporated in the Act of Uniformity as well as in the Prayer Book? "Such Ornaments of the Church, and of the Ministers thereof at all times of their Ministration, shall be retained, and be in use, as were in this Church of England by the Authority of Parliament, in the Second Year of the Reign of King Edward VI." Why this apparently clumsy circumlocution? It was not clumsy at all. It was exceedingly skilful. Elizabeth realized that in order to secure the co-operation of her Parliament she had to seem to defer to their wishes. Therefore she found a formula which lulled suspicion by emphasizing "the authority of Parliament". Thus she secured the legalization of the position which had existed *before* the First Prayer Book.[1] The law proved impossible to enforce, but Elizabeth would never sign anything which

[1] Cf. above, p. 27.

compromised the legal position she had secured. Therefore the Advertisements never became law and the Ornaments Rubric was never abrogated. But the Queen could never make the Protestants like or obey the Prayer Book. They regarded it as wholly evil and, as soon as they gained power under Cromwell, they proscribed it and made its use a penal offence. Early in Elizabeth's reign they began to express their hatred for it. It was "an unperfect Boke, culled and picked out of the Popish Dunghill the Port-wise and Masse boke, full of abominations".[1]

For political reasons the fight which developed between Catholic and Protestant was not fought to a finish in England. Everywhere else it was. In France and Spain, Italy and Germany men are either Catholics or Protestants, and know exactly for which doctrines they stand. In England although the Prayer Book, as we have seen, lends no countenance at all to the proposition that it is a Protestant compilation, Protestants continued to use it, while carrying on a constant warfare for its revision. A whole series of privately amended Prayer Books was produced between 1578 and 1640. Their general purpose can be understood in such changes as these: "priest" was replaced by "minister"; services were drastically revised to give effect to Calvinistic and Zwinglian doctrine; ceremonies such as the cross in baptism and the ring in marriage were omitted; provision for private baptism and communion of the sick was cut out. The attack from the Protestant side was pressed without any scruple or decency, or any feeling for fair play. But in spite of the fact that Parliament on the whole was favourable to the rebels, Elizabeth and her government stood firm and the attempts to remodel the Church on the Protestant pattern of Geneva, or Zurich, or Scotland utterly failed. In the end many shook its dust off their feet and went out to organize connections more in accordance with their hearts' desires. But there were left behind in the Church pockets of malcontents who, either through cowardice or worldly wisdom, did not follow the dissenters out into the Protestant wildernesses of their own making. They remained, representatives of the New Religions within the borders of the Old one, to work ceaselessly for the protestantizing of the Church of England.

[1] The "First Admonition" to Parliament.

This Protestant fifth column is still with us. Declarations are constantly being made that the Church of England comprehends many points of view and that all of them have an equal right to exist within its borders. We are told that extreme "Evangelical" Churches are as much "Church of England" as "Anglo-Catholic" ones, perhaps even more so. But this is simply not true. The contrary opinions exist, and the many customs flourish. But they ought not to do so. That is proved by the one authoritative document which the Church of England has issued—the Book of Common Prayer. Doctrines which are contrary to it are disloyal. Churches which do not obey its directions represent disloyal and rebellious elements, which the Church has never been able to subdue, which in generation after generation have tried to assimilate the doctrine and practice of the Church of England to those of Protestants, and dissenters. But denials of articles of the Creed, or of the Catechism, or heretical teaching about the Church or the Blessed Sacrament, or disobedience to the Prayer Book do not constitute loyal Churchmanship. The Church itself holds all the articles of the Catholic Faith, even if some of its members do not. It orders all its ministers to recite the Apostles' Creed twice daily. Its defined doctrine about the Blessed Sacrament is orthodox. There are not two possible interpretations of episcopacy, however loudly disloyal elements may shout that there are. There is one interpretation in the Prayer Book and all others are held in defiance of the Church of England. Turn to the Preface to the Ordinal. It makes these statements:

1. There have been bishops from the time of the Apostles.
2. Therefore the episcopal order is to be "continued" and reverently used.
3. No one is to be "suffered to execute" in the Church of England any of the functions of bishop, priest, or deacon unless he has had episcopal consecration or ordination.

To say that this propounds no theory of apostolic succession is nonsense. To say that it contains no teaching about episcopacy being of the very *esse* of the Church is equally nonsense. For the regulation says that apart from episcopacy there is to be no confirmation, no Holy Communion, no absolution, no ministerial blessing, and no ordination. The Church is to cease. If that is not teaching that bishops are essential to the very life of the Church, in the name of common sense, what is it?

There are many people working for a union of the Church of England with Presbyterians and other dissenters in England. Suppose such a union could be consummated. Suppose, further, that it could be agreed that there must be, not a federation, but a real union. All who join in the union must worship together and therefore there must be a Prayer Book which all could use. Supposing the dissenters condescended to agree that the Book of Common Prayer afforded the best basis for this United Church Prayer Book. All this does not require any very great effort of imagination. It might well happen. But suppose, further, that the task of revising the Book of Common Prayer in order to make it really acceptable throughout the United Church was then undertaken. The following quite incredible position would ensue. Such changes as these would be necessary. In the Ordinal: "It is evident unto all men diligently reading holy Scripture and ancient Authors (except to those to whom the opposite is evident), that from the Apostles' time there have been these Orders." At the Ordination of a Priest: "Unless you believe that in the Church of Christ there is no priesthood except his, Receive the Holy Ghost for the office and work of a Priest." In the Catechism: "How many Sacraments?" "Provided you do not believe that sacraments are unnecessary, two only, as generally necessary to salvation." In Holy Baptism: "Seeing now . . . that this child is regenerate (or may not be, for God alone knows who is), and grafted into the Body of Christ's Church (or may not be, because the Church being invisible its members are known only to God)." In Confirmation: "and there shall none be admitted to the holy Communion until such time as he be confirmed, or be ready and desirous to be confirmed, except in the case of those, who do not hold with confirmation." "Then shall the Bishop (or, if it be desired, some other Minister) . . . lay his hand." In Holy Matrimony: "Those whom God hath joined together let no man put asunder, save a Divorce Court Judge." However ridiculous this may seem, it is true that only by such amendments and additions as these could the Prayer Book be rendered really acceptable to Protestant separatists. It was partly on points such as these that they left the Church, and very many still remain faithful to their ancient principles. The fact that such amendments would be necessary shows up the falseness of the repeated assertion that the Protestant and Broad Church parties have as much right in the Church of England as the Catholics have. It is the Catholic alone who finds support for his views in the Prayer Book. Protestants and modernists may claim a kind of "unholy succession" from the Tudor and Stuart enemies of the Prayer Book. They may claim that the Church of England has never been able to reduce rebels to order, or to suppress them. But they cannot claim that it did not try to do so, or that it freely and gladly tolerated them. They may claim that, after the exile of the House of Stuart, when the more Catholic section of the Church left it, rather than break their oath of fidelity to the legitimate King, they obtained a stranglehold through the favour of the Protestant Hanoverian sovereigns. They may claim that in the days of their power they all but killed the Church of England. But the Prayer Book proves that they have always been traitors. They have always been a kind of fifth column, working in the interests of separatists, in both the shooting civil war of Charles I's time and the cold wars which preceded and followed it.

It is the existence of these disloyal elements which gives the Church of England the appearance of being a house divided against itself. But appearances can be very deceitful. To the orderly Germans of the Kaiser's Empire the British Empire looked to be a contemptible, ramshackle affair, certain to fall to pieces as soon as it was tried in the fire of adversity. It had no unifying organization, no legal obligations, no force to hold it together. In fact it had nothing common to all its parts but a sentimental affection for the Mother Country and the symbol of a Crown, which had been stripped of all effective power. It could not survive the strain of war. How wrong they were. Danger proved that it was one of the most solidly united forces in the world. Roman Catholics, subjects of the best organized autocracy the world has ever known, may think that the Church of England, torn by party strife, is doomed to extinction because it does not enforce obedience. But to an extent which the outsider cannot begin to understand, it attracts the love and admiration of its children. Moreover it has its "Crown", its symbol of unity, in the Book of Common Prayer, and, in spite of all appearances, that is a far more compelling force than non-Anglicans realize.

CHAPTER 20

THE OLD RELIGION

IT IS TIME to sum up. We have been considering all the foregoing matters to one end—the uncovering of the true answers to these questions: Where is the Catholic Church of England? Where is the Old Religion, the religion which St Columba and St Augustine brought to our country? Which body of bishops who claim to be their successors are justified in their claim? Are the bishops of the Roman obedience the true Catholic bishops and are the Anglican, for one reason or another, spurious? Or are the Anglican bishops the true Catholic bishops in England and the papal ones intruders? If both kinds of bishops are real bishops then one kind must be schismatic, for one or the other has set up altars in opposition to the Catholic Church of the country. There is no doubt at all that there has been no continuing Roman Catholic succession. The Pope's hierarchy ended with the death of the last Marian bishop and was not restored until 1850. On the other hand, there has been an unbroken succession of Anglican bishops ruling the ancient sees, which has continued from the medieval Church, through the troubles of the Reformation period, to the present day. Obviously *if* these have been true bishops, and *if* they have ruled over a Church which in all essentials has been Catholic in faith and practice, then it is the bishops of the unbroken, continuing, succession who are the Catholic bishops of our country, and the faithful over whom they rule are the members of the Catholic Church in England. All others must be schismatics.

We have considered in detail the claim of the Anglican bishops to be true bishops, and we have seen that, when judged by present papal standards, their claim is wholly justified. Has the body over which they have ruled been Catholic in faith and practice? It has contained many heretics, but so has every part of the Church—there was a Judas even among the apostles. The important point is not the opinion of individuals, but official faith and practice.

This question, also, has been faced in detail and we have found that in its organization the Church of England conforms to that which Catholic tradition asserts to be right. Its clergy are authorized in ample form to do all the things which are customary in the Catholic Church. Its whole ordering of the Church's year, with its changing seasons and commemorations, is that of the Catholic Church. Its standards of faith are the Scriptures, the Creeds and the acknowledged general Councils. It continued to administer the sacraments of the Catholic Church with all that is essential to their validity. It avoided the traps set by the distinctive heresies of the Protestant sects.

At the accession of Elizabeth there were 8806 parishes in England and less than 200 of the parochial clergy were deprived, so that in almost every parish the same priests carried on with duties which were obviously the same. It was because the Book of Common Prayer, which the old priests used, was recognized as a Catholic book that English papalists attended their parish churches during the early years of the Queen's reign. In 1562 they petitioned the Pope and the Council of Trent asking for formal permission to do so. The request was forwarded by the Spanish ambassador, Quadra, with a covering letter, explaining that the Prayer Book contained no impiety, or false doctrine, although what concerned the merits and intercession of the saints had been omitted. The official Latin translation of the Prayer Book (Haddon's), issued in 1560, attracted much attention in Catholic circles abroad and especially at the French Court, where there was talk of its being made the basis for a universal reform. All this is completely consistent with the report that about this time the Cardinal of Lorraine made to the English ambassador an offer that the Pope would confirm the Prayer Book, if the Queen would accept it as coming from him and would acknowledge his supremacy. Frere says "no direct documentary evidence of such a proposal is forthcoming; in delicate matters of diplomacy the crucial points are not written. But it is clear that Parpaglia [the papal envoy] had authority to go beyond his written instructions. Although written evidence is lacking until ten years later, there is reason to believe that the Pope did make such an offer. It was frequently spoken about from 1571 onwards; the queen herself talked openly of it.

The recusants of later days were eager to deny it; but this was certainly not the frame of mind of the recusants of 1562."[1]

It is neither the doctrine, nor the customs, of the Prayer Book which were, or are, the real problem. That is the papal supremacy. If the Church of England could accept that, there is very little doubt that the same kind of authorization which is accorded to the oriental Churches, their distinctive liturgies, communion in both species, married clergy and the rest, could be accorded to the Church of England. It is the theory and the practice of the Papacy which divides us still, as it did in the days of Elizabeth.

The theory that papal jurisdiction grew under the guidance of the Holy Ghost to meet a need of the Church has been condemned. Those who accept the papal supremacy must do so on the ground that by the will of God the Papacy has always possessed a universal jurisdiction over all Christians, although it is sometimes conceded that understanding of all that this implies has developed.

But it is false to say that the Scriptures provide support for this belief. As a matter of historical fact the first recorded claim to universal jurisdiction was made by a patriarch of Constantinople, known as John the Faster, and not by a Pope. Gregory the Great protested strongly against the claim, saying, "What answer wilt thou make unto Christ, who is indeed the head of the universal Church, at the trial of the Last Judgement, that thou goest about under the name of universal bishop, to subdue the whole Church of God and all the members of Christ unto thee?"[2] "Away with words that inflate vanity and wound charity."[3] Would to God that the Popes who succeeded St Gregory had remembered his words!

Once Christians have accepted the claim that the Popes, by divine appointment, are the vicars of Christ, the representatives of God on earth, no limit can be put to their authority. All temporal sovereigns must be subordinate to them. And this is exactly what the Popes claimed. Here is Pius V, speaking for them all, in the Bull in which he excommunicated Elizabeth in 1570 and so inaugurated the schism:

He that reigns in the highest, to whom has been given all power in heaven and earth, entrusted the government of the one Holy Catholic and

[1] *History of the English Church*, Vol. 5.
[2] St Gregory, *Liber IV, Ep.* 38.   [3] Kidd's *Documents*.

Apostolic Church, outside of which there is no salvation, to one man alone on the earth, namely to Peter, the chief of the apostles, and to Peter's successor, the Roman pontiff, in fullness of power. This one man he set up as chief over all nations, and all kingdoms, to pluck up, destroy, scatter, dispose, plant, build. Resting then upon the authority of him who has willed to place us . . . in this supreme throne of justice, we declare . . . Elizabeth a heretic and an abettor of heretics, and, with those that cleave to her, to have incurred the sentence of anathema and to be cut off from the unity of Christ's body. Moreover we declare her to be deprived of her pretended right to the aforesaid realm and from all dominion, dignity and privilege whatsoever. And the nobles, subjects and peoples of the said realm, who have taken an oath of any kind to her, we declare to be absolved for ever from such oath . . . and we enjoin and forbid all . . . that they presume not to obey her and her admonitions, commands and laws. All who disobey our command we involve in the same sentence of anathema.[1]

There we have not only the claim to absolute authority upon earth, but also a not extreme example of an attempt to exercise it. Never has the Papacy abated one jot of these pretensions, or withdrawn any of them. On the contrary they have been strengthened on the spiritual side, as we have seen, by the declaration of infallibility, and therefore, at least potentially, on the political side also.

But probably the worst feature of the papal claim to universal jurisdiction is the theological one. The argument is that, since the Pope is God's representative, grace flows through the Pope to the Church. To be in communion with the Pope is necessary to salvation, because to be cut off from him is to lack valid sacraments, and in consequence to be cut off from the Body of Christ and from God. The Pope has been built up into something very like a mediator between God and man. In the words of Benedict XIV, "In the whole Church the Pope is the real priest."[2] That means that all true bishops and priests throughout the whole world are no more than his delegates. They act in his name, and their acts are valid only because they possess his authorization. The Pope is the only real priest and all others are merely his assistants. Thus Pius IX could declare "alone, notwithstanding my unworthiness, I am the successor of the apostles, the Vicar of Jesus Christ; alone I have the mission to govern and direct Peter's task; I am the way,

[1] Bettenson, *Documents*.
[2] Quoted Janus.

the truth and the life."[1] To an Anglican this seems wicked blasphemy. Both to the Orthodox and to Anglicans such a claim represents a far worse declension from universal faith and practice than all the mistakes our reformers may have made put together. A saying of St Bernard is very much to the point: "What greater pride can there be, than that one man should esteem his own judgement more than the judgement of all the Church, as if he only had the Spirit of God?"[2]

It is beyond dispute that what our reformers desired to do was to abolish abuses, which the Scriptures and primitive custom showed were uncatholic, and that they had no intention whatsoever of breaking away from the unity of the Church. If it has been proved that their deeds were consistent with their aims and that they preserved the essentials of Catholic faith and practice, then the Church of England, and no other, is the Catholic Church in England, the Old Religion of our country.

[1] Quoted Quirinus, and see Appendix E.
[2] Quoted Jewel.

THE ROMAN DECREE
ON THE MATTER AND FORM OF SACRED ORDERS

CONSTITUTIO APOSTOLICA
De Sacris Ordinibus Diaconatus, Presbyteratus et Episcopatus. 1948

Pius Episcopatus

Servus Servorum Dei

Ad perpetuam rei memoriam

1. The Sacrament of Orders was instituted by Christ, the Lord: in it spiritual power is delivered and grace conferred rightly to discharge the ecclesiastical office. The Catholic faith avows that the sacrament is one and the same for the whole Church; for as our Lord Jesus Christ gave the Church but one and the same government under the Prince of the Apostles, one and the same faith, one and the same sacrifice, so he gave but one and the same treasury of the efficacious signs of grace, that is of the sacraments. Nor has the Church in the course of the centuries substituted, nor is she able to substitute, other Sacraments for those Sacraments instituted by Christ the Lord, since, as the Council of Trent teaches, the seven Sacraments of the New Law were all instituted by Jesus Christ our Lord, and no power belongs to the Church as regards the "substance of the Sacraments", that is in what, according to the eye-witnesses and sources of divine revelation, Christ the Lord himself ordained should be preserved in the sacramental sign.

2. It must however be noted as regards the Sacrament of

Orders with which we are dealing, that it has happened, notwithstanding its unity and identity which no Catholic can ever call in question, that certain variations have been added in the execution of the rite in the course of the ages, at different times and places. This indeed was the reason why theologians began to inquire which of those variations pertained to the essence of the Sacrament of Orders and which did not: and also it proved a cause of doubts and anxieties in particular cases. Again and again, therefore, the Holy See has been humbly asked that the supreme authority of the Church should at length determine what was required for validity in the conferring of Holy Orders.

3. But it is agreed by all that the Sacraments of the New Law, namely the sensible and efficient signs of invisible grace, confer grace, and effect what they signify, and signify what they effect. Now the effects which ought to be produced and therefore signified by Holy Ordination to the Diaconate, Priesthood and Episcopate, namely power and grace, are found in all the rites of the Universal Church in different times and places, to be sufficiently signified by the imposition of hands and the words determining it. Further, no one is ignorant that the Roman Church has always considered valid the Ordinations conferred by the Greek rite, without the delivery of the instruments, so that at the Council of Florence itself, when the union of the Greeks with the Roman Church was dealt with, it was by no means imposed on the Greeks that they should alter the rite of Ordination, or insert the delivery of the instruments: on the contrary the Church wished that in Rome itself the Greeks should be ordained according to their own rite. From which it may be gathered, that even according to the mind of the Council of Florence, the delivery of the instruments is not, by the will of our Lord Jesus Christ himself, required for the substance and validity of this Sacrament. If at any time by the will and decree of the Church the delivery of the instruments had also been necessary for validity, everyone knows that the Church has power to change or abrogate what she has decreed.

4. Since these things are so, having invoked the divine light, by our supreme Apostolic Authority and certain knowledge we declare, and as far as is needed, we decree and enact: the sole matter of Holy Orders for the Diaconate, the Priesthood and the

Episcopate to be the imposition of hands: the sole form also to be words determining the application of the matter, which unequivocally signify the sacramental effects—that is the power of Orders and the grace of the Holy Spirit—which are accepted as such and used by the Church. Hence it follows that we declare, so as indeed to do away with every controversy, and to close the way to scruples of conscience, we declare by our Apostolic Authority, and if at any time it has legitimately been settled otherwise, we ordain that at least in future the delivery of the instruments is not necessary for the validity of Holy Orders for the Diaconate, the Priesthood and the Episcopate.

5. Concerning the matter and form for the conferring of each Order by our same supreme Apostolic Authority, we decree and ordain what follows. In the Ordinations of Deacons the matter is the one imposition of the hand of the Bishop which occurs in this rite. The form consists in the words of the Preface, of which these are essential and therefore required for validity. "Send forth upon him, we beseech Thee, O Lord, the Holy Spirit, by whom he may be strengthened by the sevenfold gifts of Thy grace to fulfil the work of Thy ministry." In the Ordination of Priests the matter is the first imposition of the hand of the Bishop which is done in silence, but not the continuation of that imposition by the extension of the right hand, nor the last imposition to which are added the words: "Receive the Holy Spirit: whose sins ye remit, etc.": The form consists in the words of the Preface of which these are essential and therefore required for validity: "Give, we beseech Thee, almighty Father, to this thy servant the dignity of the Presbyterate; renew him with the spirit of holiness, that accepted by Thee, O God, he may hold the office worthily and win a good report by the example of his life and conversation." Lastly in Episcopal Ordination or Consecration the matter is the imposition of hands performed by the consecrating Bishop. The form consists in the words of the Preface of which these are essential and therefore required for validity: "Confer on thy Priest the highest dignity of thy ministry, and furnished with every honour, sanctify him with the dew of heavenly unction." But let everything be as was laid down by our Apostolic Constitution "Episcopal Consecration" of 30 November 1944.

6. Lest any occasion for doubt should arise, we ordain that the imposition of hands in the conferring of any Order should be by touching physically the head of the ordinand, although even moral contact suffices for the accomplishment of the Sacrament.

Finally as regards what we have decreed and laid down above about the matter and form, it is by no means to be understood as allowing the other rites laid down in the Roman Pontifical to be somewhat neglected or set aside; rather indeed we command that every rule given in the Roman Pontifical is to be faithfully observed and carried out.

The decrees of this Our Constitution have no force as towards the past; but anything doubtful is to be submitted to the Holy See.

These things we establish, declare and decree, there being no hindrances whatever, even deserving special mention, and therefore we wish and command that they shall be made evident in the Roman Pontifical. It is not lawful for any man therefore to infringe this Our Constitution secretly, nor boldly to oppose it.

Given at Rome, at St Peter's, the thirtieth day of November, on the feast of St Andrew the Apostle, in the year 1947, the ninth of Our Pontificate.

14

APPENDIX B

IN CASE any question should arise about the accuracy of the translation of the papal Decree, the original Latin of the essential points is here given.

The Matter

Divino lumine invocato, suprema Nostra Apostolica Auctoritate et certa scientia declaramus et, quatenus opus sit, decernimus et disponimus: Sacrorum Ordinum Diaconatus, Presbyteratus et Episcopatus materiam eamque unam esse manum impositionem.

The Form

In Ordinatione Presbyterali Forma autem constat verbis "Praefationis" quorum haec sunt essentialis ideoque ad valorem requisita: "Da quaesumus, omnipotens Pater, in hunc famulum tuum Presbyterii dignitatem; innova in visceribus eius spiritum sanctitatis, ut acceptum a Te, Deus, secundi meriti munus obtineat censuramque morum exemplo suae conversationis insinuet."

In Ordinatione seu Consecratione Episcopali. . . . Forma autem constat verbis "Praefationis", quorum haec sunt essentialis ideoque ad valorem requisita: "Comple in Sacerdote tuo ministerii tui summam, et ornamentis totius glorificationis instructam coelestis unguenti rore sanctifica."

N.B. It is Rome's constant accusation that the Church of England never intended to ordain "priests" in the historic and Catholic sense of the word. But the Prayer Book uses the term "Priest", and not Presbyter or Minister, whenever any traditionally priestly function is indicated. In Haddon's Latin Prayer Book, which was issued *with authority* in Elizabeth's reign, and is the only Latin Translation of the Prayer Book which has been authorized, the term "Priest" is translated *sacerdos* throughout. In the Form which the Pope has decreed to be the official form, the Roman Church contents itself with *Presbyterii dignitatem*. A Roman deacon is ordained to the presbyterate.

APPENDIX C

THE MEANING OF SACRIFICE

It is not possible to deal with this most intricate subject in a few
paragraphs, and indeed to attempt to do so would necessitate
straying far beyond the purpose of this book.[1] In my text I have
tried to do no more than indicate the forms of the doctrine with
which our reformers were confronted and to emphasize the
orthodoxy of their reactions, in the framework of the knowledge
of their times. Even from the point of view of to-day the worst
that can be said about their teaching is that, in the medieval
manner, it fixes its gaze too exclusively upon the cross, and
seeks the meaning of sacrifice too narrowly in the death of the
victim. On the other hand it has preserved *all* the elements
which "sacrifice" must comprehend. Bread and wine are offered.
They become the Body and Blood of Christ and as such they are
consumed. The representation of the death is complete. But, so
we are told, the real essence of sacrifice is to be sought in the
taking up of the victim into the life of God. This also is effected.
For the bread and wine are but the symbols of the faithful who
lay themselves on the altar. They are united to the saving Victim
by consecration and communion, so that they may evermore
"dwell in him and he in them". The Body of Christ, which
offers itself, is merged in him who ever liveth to intercede, and by
him is taken up into the life of God.

Archbishops Temple and Maclagan, when replying to Leo
XIII's condemnation of Anglican Orders, wrote:

We truly teach the doctrine of the Eucharistic Sacrifice, and do not
believe it to be a "nude commemoration of the Sacrifice of the Cross".
We continue a perpetual memory of the precious death of Christ, who is
our Advocate with the Father, and the propitiation for our sins according
to his precept until his coming again: for first we offer the sacrifice of

[1] See de la Taille, *The Mystery of Faith*, and Mascall, *Corpus Christi*.

praise and thanksgiving; then we plead and represent before the Father the Sacrifice of the Cross, and by it we confidently entreat remission of sins and all other benefits of the Lord's Passion for all the whole Church; and lastly we offer the sacrifice of ourselves to the Creator of all things, which we have already signified by the oblation of his creatures.

THE GRAMMAR OF ST MATTHEW 16.18

THE ACTUAL text of our Lord's promise to St Peter, the cause of so much controversy, requires a little consideration. In the Latin form, in which it is received by Roman Catholics, he said: "Tu es Petrus et super hanc petram aedificabo ecclesiam meam." The difficulty is that in that sentence St Peter's name is masculine and the foundation rock on which the Church is to be built, *hanc petram*, is feminine. The words can be translated quite literally as "thou art man-Peter and upon this woman-peter I will build". Or, again, "thou art stone-man and upon this female-stone I will build". *Petram* (feminine) cannot relate to *Petrus* (masculine). It must refer therefore to something which came *before* the sentence. That, as we have seen, is exactly what the Roman missal itself says. *Petram hanc* (this stone) looks back past St Peter to his confession of faith. "Thou art the Christ, the Son of the living God", is the foundation on which our Lord says he will build his Church.

Two forlorn attempts have been made to turn the flank of this argument, one by Roman Catholics in the interests of the papal claims and the other by Protestants, who do not seem to believe that our Lord founded any Church at all. Roman Catholics sometimes suggest that since Aramaic was our Lord's usual language these words must have been spoken in Aramaic and, since Aramaic has no genders, the difficulty would not have arisen. It is only when the words are translated that they become ambiguous. But there is no proof of any kind that the words were spoken in Aramaic. Sometimes our Lord quoted from the Scriptures in Hebrew. St Peter (2 Pet. 2.4–8) appears to link up this incident of his blessing with Isaiah 28.16. Therefore it is possible that our Lord spoke in Hebrew. If he did, and has been reported correctly, then the word for stone would be neuter and, as in Greek and Latin, could not have direct connection with St Peter's name.

But all this is completely empty speculation. There is not a shred of real evidence about what language our Lord used on this occasion. The contention is parallel with the futile criticism which comes from the other side. That is that our Lord never spoke the words at all! If he had done so, we are told, then one of the other evangelists, especially St Mark, would have some reference to them. Moreover the conception "build my Church" is entirely foreign to his thought. This metaphor of a building occurs nowhere else in his teaching. But this argument also is simple vanity. There is no reason why our Lord should not have used the term only once in the whole of his ministry, and there are a dozen good reasons, which can be imagined, for the silence of the other evangelists. There is no doubt that St Paul and St Peter got their conception of the Church as a building from somewhere. Why not from here? There is not the slightest real reason to doubt that our Lord spoke the words.

Both the argument based on a supposed interpolation of the text and that on a supposed use of Aramaic must be completely rejected. Why? Because although some scholars may be right, and there may be an Aramaic gospel behind St Matthew, there is no proof that this is so. We do know that once there were many accounts of our Lord's life. St Luke says so (Luke 1.1-4). But none of them has survived, except our four gospels. These, we know, were written not in Hebrew, or Aramaic, but in Greek. And these Greek scriptures received the imprimatur of the whole Church. They are presented to us by the Church as authentic as they stand. We cannot get behind the Greek, and in the Greek text which we are considering *Petros* and *Petra* are different genders. The distinction comes to us, therefore, from the very earliest version of the gospel which has survived. When St Jerome translated the Greek into Latin he faithfully reproduced this distinction.

This text, then, is presented to us by the whole Church, not in some imaginary form, but as it is actually contained in Greek and Latin in a gospel which is part of the acknowledged Canon of Scripture. That being so the whole passage can be paraphrased like this: "And Simon Peter said, Thou are the Christ the Son of the living God. And Jesus said, Blessed art thou Simon, son of Jonah, for flesh and blood hath not revealed it unto thee, but my

Father . . . and I say unto thee, thou art Rock (man) and upon this (woman) rock (which is the faith in me, which thou hast just confessed), I will build my Church. . . . Then charged he that . . . they should tell no man, that he was the Christ." Roman Catholics cannot deny this without repudiating their official attitude to the Canon of Scripture in general and to the Vulgate, their authorized Latin version, in particular. This argument holds for them even if the conclusions of Dr Cullmann are accepted by non-Romans.[1]

[1] Cullmann, *Peter, Disciple, Apostle and Martyr.*

APPENDIX E

THE CLAIM MADE BY PIUS IX

"I AM the way, the truth and the life." Roman Catholics are eager to deny that Pius IX said any such thing about himself. But the words were reported at the time in three different French newspapers and *The Times* correspondent said that the Pope "identified himself" with his master. Such an identification would actually be justified if "for every creature to be subject to the Roman Pope is altogether necessary to salvation". These official words of Boniface VIII have never been withdrawn. If they are true then the Pope must be, in a very real sense, the way to heaven. The infallible mouthpiece of the Holy Spirit must be the truth on earth. Since only those sacraments are valid which are administered by the authorization of the Pope, he must be, in a sense the life, for sacraments are necessary to salvation. Indeed, if the papal claims are justified, the Pope could truly say "no man cometh to the Father, but by me".

THE "FORM OF SUBMISSION" TO THE POPE

IT IS possible that many Anglicans are not familiar with the vow which is demanded from converts to Roman Catholicism. This is an extract from the Office for the Reception of a Convert in the *Rituale Romanum*.

I *N.M.* having before my eyes the Holy Gospels, which I touch with my hand, and knowing that no one can be saved without that faith which the Holy Catholic, Apostolic, Roman Church holds, believes and teaches ; against which I grieve that I have greatly erred, inasmuch as, having been born outside that Church, I have held and believed doctrines opposed to her teaching. I, now enlightened by the grace of God, profess that I believe the Holy, Catholic, Apostolic, Roman Church to be the one true Church, established on earth by Jesus Christ, to which I submit myself with my whole heart. I firmly believe all the articles that she proposes to my belief; I reject and condemn all that she commands me. And especially I profess that I believe One only God . . . the primacy, not only of honour but also of jurisdiction of the Roman Pontiff, successor of St Peter, prince of the apostles, vicar of Jesus Christ . . . with a sincere heart therefore, and with unfeigned faith I detest and adjure any error, heresy and sect opposed to the said Catholic Apostolic and Roman Church. So help me God and these holy gospels which I touch with my hand.

The "articles that she proposes to my belief" include the Nicene Creed, and also the dogmas of papal infallibility, the immaculate conception and the assumption of our Lady. To make the acceptance of these novelties a necessary condition of communion is an act of disloyalty to the Catholic Church.

INDEX

COUNCILS TO WHICH REFERENCE HAS BEEN MADE:

CPSIA information can be obtained
at www.ICGtesting.com
Printed in the USA
LVHW081510160419
614370LV00024B/360/P